God's Unfailing Integrity!

God remains persuaded about the success of _your_ redemption in Christ Jesus; He cannot deny Himself!

I0171792

Rudi Louw

1

Table of Contents

The Marvel of the Holy Bible

1. Uninterrupted Theme and Inspired Thought

It took *1,500 years* to compile the Holy Bible, involving *more than 40 different authors*. <u>Yet</u> the theme and inspired thought of Scripture continues *uninterrupted* from author to author, from beginning till end.

2. Absence of Mythical Stories

Compare philosophies and theories about creation in the Middle East, Europe, Asia, Africa, and Latin America and you'll find mythical scenarios: gods feuding and cutting up other gods to form the heavens and the earth, etc.

In ancient Greek mythology, Atlas carries the earth on his shoulders. In India, Hindus believe eight elephants carry the earth on their backs.

But in contrast, Job, the oldest book in the Holy Bible, declares that, *"God suspends the earth on nothing."* (Job 26:7)

This was said millennia before Isaac Newton discovered the invisible laws of gravity that delicately balance every planet and sun in its individual circuit.

In sharp contrast to every other ancient attempt to give a creation account, *the Holy Bible pictures the creation of the earth in a very scientific manner.*

For example: In Genesis Chapter One, the continents are lifted from the seas, then vegetation is formed and later animal life, all reproducing *'according to its own kind', **thus recognizing the fixed genetic laws.*** In addition, we have the bringing forth of man and woman, *all done by God in a dignified and proper manner, without mythological adornments.*

The balance or remainder of the Holy Bible follows suite.

*The narratives are **true historical documents**, faithfully reflecting society and culture **as history and archaeology would discover them thousands of years later. Not only is the Holy Bible historically accurate, it is also reliable when it deals with scientifically proven subjects.***

It was never intended to be a textbook on history, science, mathematics, or medicine. *However, when its writers touch on these subjects, **they often state facts that scientific advancement would not reveal, or***

6

even consider, until thousands of years later.

While many have doubted the accuracy of the Holy Bible, time and continued research have consistently demonstrated that the Word of God is better informed than its critics.

3. Intactness

Of all the ancient works of substantial size, *the Holy Bible survives intact, against all odds and expectations.*

Compared with other ancient writings, the Holy Bible has more manuscripts as evidence to support it than any ten pieces of classical literature combined!

The plays of William Shakespeare, for instance, were written about four hundred years ago, after the invention of the printing press. Many of his original writings and words have been lost in numerous sections, *yet the Holy Bible's uncanny preservation has weathered thousands of years of wars, contradictions, persecutions, fires and invasions.*

Through the centuries Jewish scribes have preserved the Holy Bible's Old Covenant text, ***such as no other manuscripts have ever been preserved. They kept tabs on every letter, syllable, word and paragraph.*** *They* *continued from generation to generation to appoint and train special groups of men within their culture* **whose sole duty it was to preserve and transmit these documents <u>with perfect accuracy and fidelity</u>.**

Who ever bothered to count the letters, syllables, or words of Plato, Aristotle, or Seneca for that matter?

When it comes to the New Testament, the actual number of preserved manuscripts is so great that it becomes overwhelming. *There are more than 5,680 Greek manuscripts, more than 10,000 Latin Vulgate manuscripts and at least 9,300 other versions. Further still, there exists an additional 25,000 manuscript copies of portions of the New Testament.* **No other document of antiquity even begins to approach such numbers.**

The closest in comparison is Homer's <u>Iliad</u>, with only 643 manuscripts. The first complete work of Homer only dates back to the 13th century.

4. Unmatched Accuracy in Predictive Foretelling

The Holy Bible is unmatched in accuracy in predictive foretelling. No other ancient work succeeds in this, or even begins to attempt this.

Other books such as the Koran, the Book of Mormon, and parts of the Veda claim divine inspiration; *but none of these books contain predictive foretelling.*

This one undeniable fact we know for certain: *While microscopic scrutiny would show up the imperfections, blemishes, and defects of any work of man, <u>it magnifies the beauties and perfection of God</u>. Just as every flower displays in accurate detail the reflection and perfection of beauty, <u>so does the Word of Truth when it is scrutinized</u>.*

Historian Philip Schaff wrote:

"Without money and weapons, Jesus the Christ conquered more millions than Alexander, Caesar, Muhammad, and Napoleon. Without science and learning, He (Jesus the Christ) shed more light on things human and divine than all philosophers and scholars combined. Without the eloquence of schools, He (Jesus the Christ) spoke such words of life as was never spoken before or since and produced effects which lie beyond the reach of orator or poet. Without writing a single line, He (Jesus the Christ) set more pens in motion and furnished themes for more sermons, orations, discussions, learned volumes, works of art, and songs of praise **than the whole army of great men of ancient and modern times combined.***" (The Person of Christ, p33. 1913)*

Today, there are literally billions of Bibles in more than 2,000 languages.

Isn't it about time you find out what it really has to say?

Hey listen, the Holy Bible is all about Jesus, the Messiah, the Christ…

…and everything about Jesus Christ is really about YOU!!

Study Tips:

Read 2 Corinthians 5:14, 16, 18, 19, and 21.

In the light of these Scriptures, it should be obvious that, if you want to study the Holy Bible, *you should study it in the light of Mankind's redemption!*

Feed daily on **redemption realities** found in the book of Acts, in Romans Chapters One through Eight, and in Ephesians, Colossians, and Galatians. These realities are also found in 1 Peter Chapter One, 2 Peter Chapter One, James Chapter One, as well as in 1 and 2 Corinthians.

Foreword

Thank you for taking the time to read this book.

Let me start off by saying that *I am totally addicted to my Daddy's love for me.*

I am in love with Jesus Christ, *and that is enough for me!*

The love of God is so much more than a doctrine, a philosophy, or a theory. It is so much more and goes so much deeper than knowledge; *it way surpasses knowledge.* **We are talking heart language here.**

Thus, I write *to impact people's hearts,* to make them see the mysteries that have been hidden in Father God's heart concerning Christ Jesus, and actually *concerning THEM,* so as to arrest their conscience with it, *that I may introduce them to their original design and to their true selves,* **and present them to themselves perfect in Christ Jesus** *and set them apart unto Him **in love**,* as a chaste virgin.

We are involved with the biggest romance of the ages. Therefore this book cannot be read as you would a novel: *casually.* It is not a cleverly devised little myth or fable. **It contains revelation and *truth* into some things you may or may not have considered before.**

It is *the TRUTH of God, ultimate TRUTH, and therefore has direct bearing upon YOUR life.* The Word and the Spirit are my witness *to the reality of these things!*

Be like the people of Berea the apostle Paul ministered to in Acts 17:11. Open yourself up to study the revelation contained in this book *to discover for yourself the reality of these things*.

Be forewarned! Do not become guilty of the sins of the Pharisees, **or you too will miss out on the depth of fulfillment God Himself, who is LOVE, wants to give you**.

Jesus said of the Pharisees and Sadducees that they strain out every little gnat BUT swallow whole camels. What He meant by that is that *some people seem to have it all together when it comes to doctrine and they love to argue.* **It makes them feel important, but it is nothing other than EMPTY religious and intellectual pride.** *They know the Scriptures in and out, and YET they are still so IGNORANT about* **REAL TRUTH that is only found in LOVE.** They are always arguing over the use of *every little jot and tittle* and over the meaning and interpretation of **every word of Scripture,** *but they are still so ignorant and indifferent t***owards the things that REALLY MATTER!**

The exact thing they accuse everyone else of doing though, the precise thing they judge everyone else for, *they are actually doing themselves.* That is **they often downright misinterpret and twist what is being said, *making a big deal of insignificant things while obscuring or weakening God's real truth: the truth of His LOVE.*** They are always majoring on minors **<u>because they do not understand the heart of God</u> and therefore they constantly miss the whole point of the message**.

Paul himself said it so beautifully,

*"...the letter kills but **the Spirit BRINGS LIFE;"***

*"...<u>knowledge puffs up</u>, but **LOVE EDIFIES**."*

I say again:

Allow yourself to get caught up in the revelation I am about to share. Open yourself up to study the insight contained in this book, *not only with a desire to gain knowledge, but also with anticipation **to hear from Father God yourself;***

...to encounter Him through His Word;

...and to embrace truth, in order to know and believe the LOVE God has for <u>you</u>, *so that you may get so caught up in it,* ***that you too may receive from Him LOVES' impartation of LIFE.***

This revelation contains within it the voice and call of LOVE Himself to every human being on the face of this earth. *If you take heed to it, it is custom designed and guaranteed to forever alter and enrich your life!*

Acknowledgment

I want to acknowledge and thank one of my mentors in the faith, Francois du Toit, for blessing and impacting me with revelation knowledge.

I borrowed the portion on *"The Marvel of the Holy Bible"* from his website: http://www.MirrorWord.net, as students so often feel they have a right to do with things that come from teachers they respect. Just as Galatians 6:6 says, *"Let him who is taught the Word **share in all good things** with him who teaches."*

To all our dear friends and family, for all the love and support, and to Chase Aderhold and all those who helped me with this project:

THANK YOU!

Also, especially to my wife, Carmen;

For keeping me real by being my companion in life and partner in ministry,

I love and appreciate you so very much!

"For what if some did not
believe?
Will their unbelief
nullify the integrity of God?
Will it
prove God unfaithful?

By no means!

Indeed,
let God be true
but every man a liar!

For it is written:
You will be justified

in Your words,
and will overcome
if You are judged."
~ Romans 3:3-4

"Abraham did not waver
at the promise of God
through unbelief,
but was strengthened in faith,
while giving glory to God;
being fully persuaded
that what He had promised
He was then also able to make
real.

And therefore,
"It was accounted to him for
righteousness."

Now it was not written for his
sake alone
that it was imputed to him,
but also for us.

It shall be imputed to us
who believe in Him

who raised up Jesus our Lord
from the dead,

He (Jesus) was delivered up
by and for our offenses,
and was raised
because of our justification."
— Romans 4:20-25

Prayer

As I bow my heart before you today Father, it is with an overwhelming consciousness and awareness of the greatness and the splendor of Your presence; *of Your nearness!*

Thank you that You have brought us into Your bosom. We were outside, but now we are inside, thanks to You!

Thank you Father that we are no longer afar off, *we have been brought near by the blood of Christ!*

We have been brought near in Your love!

Father, we just so appreciate Your love today!

We simply appreciate *what You have poured out and awakened in our hearts.*

We appreciate the large measure of Your love, and the measure of Your Spirit attached to that love, which has come into our spirits to abide there, *in that same full measure as the large revelation of Your love!*

We also therefore appreciate today the measure of Your word; *the measure of Your working within us,*

We appreciate the largeness and clarity of Your message in the gospel; the largeness and clarity of revelation-knowledge, *equipping us!*

Thank you for what You see, in every person, and especially for what You see, in every believer, in every saint; *in us, as your ambassadors!*

Thank you for what You see, in Your children, in the human race, *in each and every son of Yours,* **whether they have embraced sonship yet or not!**

Thank you Lord!

Amen!

Hallelujah!

Chapter 1

Nothing Can Nullify God's Intention, Or Faithfulness!

What God has to say to us in Christ, in the gospel, in the work of redemption is so good and so rich, I am sure the dictionaries are going to run out of words soon, ha… ha… ha… unless we create new words, ha… ha… ha…

…because I don't know about you, but the more I appreciate and esteem *what God esteems* in His Word, *and in us,* the more I find myself hunting for words, to somehow find the perfect expression, the perfect definition …*to somehow try and capture my innermost thoughts, and capture the experience of my spirit **lavishing and just indulging in the glory of God.***

Praise God for words and for languages and for these vehicles of communication we have today in our hands and in our mouths *by which we can capture the truth God is revealing to us **of Himself and of us!***

You know, the more I get caught up in His goodness, and in His person, and in His nearness, *the more I realize that there is often an experience that God intends for us as His body to enjoy, that goes beyond words.*

23

I believe it is what Paul had in mind to try and communicate and convey to us in Romans 8:26 when he speaks of that place of communion in the Holy Spirit and joint-prayer with Him …where He begins to intercede in your spirit with passion and groaning and feelings and yearnings and deep desires for oneself and for others *which cannot be uttered*

The Greek literally says that it is *unutterable.*

There is no vocabulary for it, to be able to give expression to it, *to give sufficient expression of it, to give adequate expression, full expression to it.* But your spirit responds and comes in agreement with it *and finds expression for it elsewhere if it has to, even perhaps in your emotions if need be.*

Paul is not just speaking about speaking in other tongues, what he has written here in this passage of Scripture speaks of something that is above and beyond speaking in tongues.

Praise God for speaking in tongues, it's wonderful, it's another means of explosion and communion and communication and utterance *for your spirit to be able to speak in a language that goes beyond the limits and the words of a natural vocabulary …but this communion which Paul is talking about here, this communication within your heart by the Spirit of God goes even deeper.*

It is a groaning and an intensity of spirit encounter and experience *in direct fellowship and communion with God; with*

24

His thoughts and with His heart and with His Spirit and with His person!

It speaks of an absolute union and oneness with God, being in union with God, absolute union of spirit, and sharing oneness with God, *where I am one with Him and He is one with me.*

It is a groaning and intensity of spirit *that comes out of* **absolute oneness of fellowship and oneness of heart!**

It is a groaning and intensity of spirit that *is in fact generated and inspired by that fellowship within the heart of God;* it comes from *"KONONIA."*

In fact, appreciating what God appreciates *is the basis of faith and encounter!*

As I appreciate what God appreciates, it becomes the basis of faith for me, amen!

It becomes my place of encounter!

I have another book written on the subject of being *fully persuaded.*

Now being *fully persuaded* **is being under that complete influence of God's persuasion.**

It's a spirit thing; *not just a mental thing!*

It is nothing short of **esteeming God's own unwavering confidence** *in His word, in His truth, in His gospel message;* **in what He has to say to us in Christ**, *in the incarnation and* *work of redemption that culminates in the resurrection and ascension of Man, of us, in Christ Jesus.*

Our faith is our appreciating or our esteeming of *God's own unwavering confidence in that word!*

…in His Word!

Hallelujah!

And so you see, the more we focus our inner-man, our spirit-man *to see the reality of God's intention,* **the more that faith builds into our spirit** *a persuasion, a confidence that is unwavering.*

Hallelujah!

To have faith, *to have strong faith is* **to discover for yourself***…* **Faith is:** *Discovering God's estimation of us, of me, of you, in Christ Jesus.*

As in almost all my books we are going to focus in on that; *because it is the greatest discovery one can ever come to!*

I want us to see in the Scriptures, **God's integrity.**

…so that His integrity becomes <u>the fuel of our faith</u>*!*

Hallelujah!

Let's start by going to Hebrews 4:2

"…for good news came to us, just as to them, but the word which they heard did not benefit them, because it did not meet with faith in the hearers."

The Greek text actually says,

*"…**it did not mix together with faith in the hearts of the hearers**."*

A word, a message came to us, just as to them.

God's words came to us just as to them. God's word, God's mighty vehicle of His intention with Man, that mighty vehicle of God's purpose came to us, just as it did to them.

It came to us; it came to the whole world, *but where it did not mix together with faith … wherever the word did not find, in the heart of Man, the response of faith and integrity, **it failed then, and it fails now, to benefit that individual**.*

I say again: *Wherever the word does not find, in the heart of the hearer, the appropriate reverence, the appropriate response of faith and integrity, **it fails to benefit the individual**.*

In other words: **The truth of God you refuse to embrace as truth is the truth that fails to benefit you!**

Now, if you have your Bible with you, turn with me to Romans Chapter 3. If not, just keep reading, *but I want you to pay close attention to what is being said* in Romans 3.

In verse 3, Paul makes this statement, *"…but if some were unfaithful,* **does their faithlessness nullify the faithfulness of God?***"*

"…but if some were unfaithful…"

Would you agree with me that if that *unfaithfulness* refers to anything, **it would refer to the exact Scripture we have just read?**

…**where the word that came to them did not benefit them,** *because they did not embrace it in their hearts and did not mix it together with the appropriate faith!*

That is exactly what their unfaithfulness was all about, *and that then is also the unfaithfulness Paul is talking about here in Romans 3:3.*

You see, it is absolutely vital for the word, for the truth of the gospel, _to be cemented in us, in our hearts_, by that ingredient and degree of spirit appreciation necessary to release the fullness of God's intention in that word.

But Paul asks us now whether that unfaithfulness, (that disbelief, and unbelief), or even people's experience in the now, **nullify God's integrity?**

No, not at all!

Does another person's experience of failure nullify God's intention with Me?

No, it does not!

It cannot!

Verse 4 says,

"By no means!"

So Paul says to you here, in other words,

"Listen man, another person's faithlessness, another person's unfaithfulness can never nullify or make void the faith of God."

"It can never make void the faithfulness of God."

He says,

"By no means!"

So, don't you ever think that Man will ever get it right *to prove God unfaithful.*

It is never going to happen!

"Let God be true, as it is written, though every man be false!"

In other words,

"Let God be found true, let God be found right, let God be found genuine and trustworthy, unfailing in His integrity …even if every person on this planet is proven to be false, is proven to be fake, or proven to be wrong …even if every person on this planet fail to embrace and appreciate, and appropriately respond to God's word, to God's integrity,

to what God has said and declared and revealed and made available for us to enjoy!"

Paul says,

"Let God be true, though every man be proven false ...Let God be true, just as it is written…"

He says,

"…it is written; that God will be justified in His words, and prevail when He is judged."

In other words,

"…whatever is written, is written so that God may be justified in His words, and therefore He prevails when He is judged."

That means, no man's argument will hold water, *because the truth, as God has declared it,* **is on record.**

It is recorded **thoroughly enough for us to comprehend it and understand it!**

It is recorded **thoroughly enough to refute and defeat every argument against it!**

Hallelujah!

"God will be justified in His words, and He will prevail when He is judged!"

"Let God be true, though every man be false!"

Let me tell you something, I am so glad that God can face any size crisis.

God can face crisis head on *and remain immovable!*

Hallelujah! Ha... ha... ha...

You see, that *is the bottom line of integrity!*

The bottom line of integrity is *whether crisis can be faced or not!*

Let's quickly look also at Romans 9:3-6.

Paul says in Verse 3,

"I could wish that I myself were accursed and cut off from Christ for the sake of my brethren, my kinsman by race…"

Paul is not just playing around with words here; he does not waste words when he writes.

No, he fully understands that being of this specific race, the Jewish race, *there is a specific privilege attached to that race; Covenant promises;* **Covenant integrity!**

But the word did not benefit them!

Look at Romans Chapter 10:1

"Brethren, my heart's desire and prayer to God, for them, is that they may be saved (rescued)."

*"I bear them witness that they have a zeal for God …**but it is not enlightened …for being ignorant of the righteousness that comes***

31

*from God, and therefore still seeking to establish their own, **they did not submit** to God's righteousness"*

Let's go back to verse 4 of Romans Chapter 9.

It says, *"They are Israelites …my kinsman by race …they are my brethren,"*

Amen, **they are our** *brethren.*

The gospel came to them, just as it came to us.

That means, **the same intention that God had for the Jew, He had for the gentile***, praise the Lord.*

All the earth, every tribe, every tongue, every nation, every race, every ethnic group **was included in God's love-dream, and in God's redemption work.**

And so Paul writes here,

"They are Israelites, and to them belong the sonship, the glory, the covenant, the giving of the law... (He is referring to the law of liberty here now, because he is talking in New Testament terms, so he is not referring to the Law of Moses here, but the perfect law of liberty, the law of identification, the law of faith.) *…to them belong the sonship, and the glory, and the covenant …thus to them belong the giving of that law* (the law of faith)*, the worship awakened by that law,* (the KONONIA, the deep intimate fellowship; **the romance of the**

ages), *and the exceedingly great and precious promises…"*

He basically says that **they should have grasped it; they should have gotten it by now,** because,

"…to them belonged all the patriarchs, and of their race, according to the flesh, is the Christ…"

Can you just imagine?

"…of their race is the Christ"

They are part of it all, just through natural descent!

Therefore, they really have no excuse; *they really should have no excuse not to embrace the gospel!*

*"God, **who is over <u>all</u>**, be blessed forever, amen!"*

He doesn't stop preaching there, he carries on in verse 6.

He says, *"**But it is not as though the word of God had failed!**"*

Just because a people or a person fails to appreciate and esteem God's intention, does not nullify God's word!

It does not nullify God's purpose!

It does not nullify or cancel God's integrity!

Amen! Hallelujah!

Chapter 2

Challenging The Weakness In Mankind!

We are living in a time when many believers have been greatly shaken to their core, because time and time again great men and leaders, who have made big names for themselves in ministry, have turned out to be a disappointment to the very message they preach.

But I really believe that it is time for us as believers *to take our eyes off of men.*

It truly is past time for us *to begin to understand* **God's integrity, independent of Man's achievement.**

When you begin to **really grasp these things** *deep down in your bosom, in your heart of hearts, in your spirit,* you will no longer be shaken in your faith, and use another person's failure as your own excuse for failure!

That means, **you will not be shaken**, *regardless of what others do,* whether they are so-called leaders or not!

Your faith will not be shaken, but instead *you will remain steadfast and immovable*

…always abounding in the knowledge of Him and in the work of the ministry!

Ha... ha... ha... Thank you Jesus!

Amen! Hallelujah!

Alright, now let's go to 2 Corinthians 13:3.

You see ministry will always be the target of the enemy.

He will always seek to somehow hamper the purpose of God through Man's fallibility.

Therefore, he always comes against God's plan with Man *and tries to snare Man **and use Man's failure** …and he tries to raise all kinds of criticisms and suspicions **against the integrity of the word.***

You see, when God entered into covenant; He entered into covenant with Himself; with the Son, and that Son took on flesh, thus, God entered into covenant with a man called Jesus, an infallible human being *who is the rest of the human race's original authentic blue-print representative.*

He proceeded from the Godhead and He took on flesh; He was a part of the triune Godhead, but He was a man, a human being, as well! He was an infallible human being, but He was a human being nonetheless.

But you see He was also more than that.

He was in very essence, God. God of very God!

36

And so the Scripture says, *"...and He Himself likewise then also partook of flesh and blood"* (Hebrews 2:14)

Why?

To give guarantee to His integrity, the kind of guarantee that could never ever be challenged!

Now Paul writes here in 2 Corinthians 13:3 and he says,

*"…since you desire **proof** that Christ is speaking in me…"*

Does that sound familiar?

I will hear you out, sir, *and if I find enough proof,* then **maybe** I'll support you!

Paul says,

"He is not weak in dealing with you, but is powerful in you."

A more accurate translation reads,

"He is not weak towards you, but mighty within you."

"For He was crucified in weakness, but lives by the power of God."

Paul has a new appreciation of weakness and power.

Look at the previous Chapter with me if you will; there in 2 Corinthians 12:8.

Remember how he sought the Lord and beseeched Him, 3 times no less, to remove this messenger of Satan sent against him.

But the Lord said to him, *"My grace is your sufficiency! For My power is made perfect in weakness!"*

Now I want us, in our study in this book, *to challenge the weakness that is in Man* **with God's power; with God's virtue.**

And I want to suggest to you that as you read this book *and determine in your heart to absorb this teaching,* that any area of weakness that perhaps has ever kept you intimidated in your own life personally, *will be outright challenged* **through God's integrity!**

God is able through His word, through the truth of the Gospel revealed and written down in the Scriptures, *to bring you into a place of power and strength and ability in Him!*

All this happens when you realize through His word, through revelation, that *your sufficiency has got nothing to do with your own flesh and your own ability.*

So, Paul speaks here in these scriptures we are looking at of the **proof of the cross** of Jesus Christ that was also something of weakness.

I mean, Jesus hung there in absolute apparent weakness and defeat.

He was so heavy laden with our iniquities and with our guilt and with our scorn.

What He went through physically was so much to endure.

He was so despised.

He was so rejected.

He was so weakened in His flesh.

He died in weakness.

BUT He was raised by the power of God!

"Examine yourselves," verse 5 of 2 Corinthians 13… *"Now examine yourselves, **to see whether you are holding to the faith**…"*

Listen don't take the faith for granted; *don't take God's faith for granted.*

"Examine yourself …test yourself..."

For what purpose?

To make sure that your faith now, not God's faith, but your faith, does not become something phony.

Paul does not write this so that you can find ground to, you know, *condemn yourself.*

No! He wants you to discover *the wealth that is yours* in Christ; he wants you to discover *the very faith of God* for yourself, and thus also, that <u>wealth</u> which He has already deposited within your inner-man.

So, don't approach that verse with a negative connotation, with a condemnation type of mentality.

Thinking, *'Oh yeah, I'm going to just suppose that I am just a failure, so I am going to quickly test myself to see if it is still so …oh, you see, I knew it, I didn't even have to take the exam, the test didn't even take long before I discovered how much of a failure I am!'*

No, listen *that is not what God through Paul was looking for you to do!*

He wants you to draw from the inexhaustible resource; **from the infallibility of the integrity of the word, from the ultimate truth of the gospel, *which reveals the wealth and fullness of Christ to be <u>within you</u>!***

So don't let your faith be just another principle that you carry around in your pocket ready to be pulled out and used *only when you absolutely need it.*

No, make a demand upon that which Christ Jesus by His Spirit *already deposited within you* of Himself.

Don't let your life just be something of a natural existence.

Here you are, and you live your whole day, *drawing from natural resources* …drawing from your senses, and from your intellect and intelligence; from your soul …and drawing from your experiences and from your natural

40

identity and from your conversations and interactions with others.

But listen, God says, *draw from your faith!*

...Draw from that knowledge of who you are, who you really are in Him, who you are as a child of your Father in heaven, *who you are in that unseen realm of spirit reality!*

Don't let the faith of who you are and of who your true Daddy is, lie there dormant!

I say again: **Don't let your faith lie dormant in your spirit!**

Paul says, *"Examine ...hold the faith up before you ...and then hold **your** faith in your hands also. ...**Bring it to mind** in other words; **bring the faith of God to mind,** and then bring your own faith in the faith of God to mind also, and **hold fast to it**. Hold fast to the faith of God; hold fast to your own faith also, **because of what you see in the faith of God!"***

He says,

*"Test yourself ...**put that knowledge to work ...put your faith to action!"***

*"Test yourself, **do you not realize that Christ is within you?"***

Do you see the object of that test?

What is the goal of this test?

To discover how much of God is deposited within me, *so that I can draw from that,*

…so that I can draw from Him!

*God wants me to **discover** how much of God is already deposited within me as a **reality,***

*…so that I can draw from Him, **from His ability;** and not the weakness of my own attempts.*

Philemon verse 6 says that,

*"…our **fellowship;** the ingredients of our KONONIA (in the Greek), **our intimate fellowship with God and with one another** is the end result, the direct result, of **the acknowledgment of every deposit; the full acknowledgment of everything that is already deposited within us,** …the recognition and acknowledgment **of every good thing that is in us**, in our union with Christ Jesus."*

Paul also writes in Hebrews 6:11 and he expresses his desire, based on God's own desire, *"**that each one of us** will show the same earnestness **in realizing** <u>the full assurance of hope</u> until the end."*

There is a realizing that comes as I constantly draw from that energy that I know is mine in Christ Jesus.

There is an actual realizing in practical reality of the Christ that is within me.

Christ within me becomes more than just a Bible doctrine; it becomes the truth, and the very Person, which energizes my whole life!

"...Christ within me!"

"...Unless, indeed, you fail at that test,"

"...Unless, indeed, you fail to realize that truth; that reality," Paul says in 2 Corinthians 13:5.

In verse 6 He says, (2 Corinthians 13:6),

"I hope you will not fail!"

"I hope you move on, and out, with the results you find!"

"...so that we have not failed in our bringing the true message to you!"

He started in verse 3, (2 Corinthians 13:3), by saying,

"Since you desire proof that Christ is speaking in us..."

He says,

"In believing these things; and testing yourselves to fully discover these things..."

"Our hope is that you will indeed find out for yourself that we have not failed."

He says,

"I hope that as you begin to draw for yourselves also from the fullness of the

43

Christ within you, *then you will have all the* *proof* *you need of the success of our ministry!"*

He says,

"…as you begin to draw from that life source within you, from that reality within you, from the fullness of the Christ-life, from Christ Himself within you, you will discover that we all live out of the same energy, out of the same source of life and ministry!"

"…so that we will all be united in the same mind and the same judgment, the same conclusion, the same persuasion, the same faith,"

"…and the same expression also, in life and in ministry"

...inspired and energized and empowered by the same true gospel, and the same indwelling Christ; the same indwelling Holy Spirit.

And now he says here, verse 7, (2 Corinthians 13:7),

"But we pray to God that you may not do wrong."

You see quite often, believers, well-meaning believers *use their suspicion about somebody else's integrity* **as a good excuse for their own failure.** What I am saying is that they would, in the weakness of their own minds, through their suspicion; *they would seek to use that suspicion as an excuse for their own sin.*

And this is exactly what Paul is getting at.

He says,

"We pray to God that you may do no wrong!"

"Not so that we may appear to have met the test, but that you may do what is right!"

"Though we may seem to have failed"

In other words, don't line up all the historic evidence of how many great men failed, and then say,

*'Well, there you have it, that's all the proof I need that the gospel doesn't work; that the truth of the gospel is not enough to deliver me and set me free; so, **that's enough justification for my weaknesses***'

*"No, brother, if you want to have proof that is of any virtue, and worth holding on to, **then look at the proof of the resurrection, and hold on to that** and say, '**That's my confidence!** My confidence is not based on, or influenced by any man! **I don't care what their experience of failure says to me! In the resurrection there is enough integrity revealed, enough proof for me to stand on!** I am not going to build my faith on somebody else's failure! **I am going to build my faith on Jesus's triumph!**"*

"…that you may do what is right, though we may seem to have failed"

Paul says in verse 8, (2 Corinthians 13:8),

"For we can't do anything against the truth, but only for the truth!"

Ha... ha... ha... What a statement!

The truth remains unchallenged!

The truth of God cannot be challenged!

We can do nothing to change it!

"…we can do nothing against the truth,"

"…only for the truth!"

Ha... ha... ha... Hallelujah!

It is not as though the word has failed.

Amen?!

It hasn't!

The word is infallible!

Incorruptible!

The word doesn't fail; *we do!*

…when we choose not to fully believe it!

Chapter 3

Let This Conclusion Be Yours!

Let's go to 1 Corinthians Chapter 1.

Now, just for some background here. Paul sits down and he writes this letter to a church that had apparent failure in their midst. One of their key members had been caught in the act of adultery.

One can just imagine Paul's disappointment in his spirit, when he realizes that these people *who have been called out of darkness into God's marvelous light,* there they are, sinning.

Now notice Paul's approach to this church.

He knows that his own inner consciousness, and his confidence has to stay focused *upon the integrity of God's grace, upon the integrity of God's redemption; upon the integrity of God's word in Christ!*

And listen; when we speak about God's grace, we do not refer to God's ability to put up with our sin, no, *we are speaking about what God legally did in the work of redemption, in His Son's death on man's behalf, to set you completely free!* Otherwise you see, grace just becomes another overdraft facility, you know, like at your local bank, *and we just kind of live* in the red all the time and say, "Praise God, He is gracious …**so let's sin** so that grace may abound"

Very convenient …**very deceived!**

Paul says,

*"**By no means!**"* (Romans 6:1 & 2)

Don't you dare use Jesus' triumph as an excuse for your weakness!

In verse 1 of 1 Corinthians 1 he starts off and he says,

"Grace (belongs) to you, and peace, from God our Father and the Lord Jesus Christ"

In verse 4, He says,

*"**I give thanks to God, always, for you!**"*

What was there in this church that would possibly encourage Paul?

God's very deposit; God's love gift!

Paul says,

*"I give thanks, always, for you, **because of the grace of God which was given you in Christ Jesus!**"*

*"…**so that, in every way, you were enriched in Him,**"*

"…with all speech and all knowledge,"

*"…even as **the testimony of Christ** was confirmed among you, and within you,"*
48

*"…so that, **you are not lacking** in any spiritual gift, as you **wait** for the revealing of* (…as you KAVAH (in the Hebrew), **as you intertwine yourself with the revelation of**) *our Lord Jesus Christ, **who will then also <u>sustain you</u> to the end, <u>guiltless</u>,** in the **day** of* (…**in the light of; in the revealed truth of**) *our Lord Jesus Christ!"*

Wow, what confidence Paul has!

*"...**who will <u>sustain you</u> to the end**..."*

*"…**<u>guiltless</u>!**"*

Paul **reminds** this church, who might be a little apprehensive by the time they receive this letter, saying to themselves, *"Uh-oh, here it is, Paul's heard all about this, and he's going to let us have it,"*

But instead, Paul **reminds** them of the truth of the gospel, *…he immediately ministers to them, from the strength of his own confidence in the integrity of God; from the strength of his faith in the ability of God to be faithful to His word; from the strength of his persuasion in the truth of the gospel, and in the ability of God* **to sustain them, <u>guiltless</u> to the end,** by that truth.

Ha... ha... ha... Isn't that wonderful?!

Sustained ...<u>guiltless</u> to the end.

Now that's a very long time!

Why does he say this?

Because of verse 9, (1 Corinthians 1:9),

"God is faithful…"

Listen, **God is faithful!**

Would Man's faithlessness nullify God's faithfulness?

God remains faithful!

*"Let every person be a liar; **God is faithful!**"*

God remains faithful!

God's faith remains full!

God is unchallenged!

I like that word, *"unchallenged"*

…unchallenged confidence!

Verse 9, (1 Corinthians 1:9),

*"**God is faithful, by whom you were called into the fellowship of His Son**, Jesus Christ, our Lord"*

"…the fellowship of the Son"

The same fellowship; the same KONONIA as the Son Himself enjoys with the Father, **the same fellowship, *nothing inferior*!**

You have been called into that, amen, hallelujah!

Ha... ha... ha... Glory!

Now Paul begins to come with his appeal, verse 10, (1 Corinthians 1:10),

"I appeal to you, brethren, by the name (by the reputation) of our Lord Jesus Christ,"

"…that all of you agree (with the truth revealed in Jesus)*,"*

"…and that there be no dissensions among you,"

*"…but that you be united, **in the same mind,** and **therefore also the same judgment*** (the same conversation and ultimate conclusion in the truth of the gospel)*,"*

*"...**the same mind**"*

What kind of mind?

What kind of judgment is he referring to?

Paul's mind and Paul's judgment.

Where did Paul get his mind form?

Where did Paul get his judgment from?

He got it from the mind of Christ; from Jesus *revealing the mind of God!*

He got it from dwelling in the truth of God's faithfulness; *from dwelling in the truth of God's integrity!*

Paul's mind, and Paul's conclusion *is **Christ's mind**, it is **God's own ultimate conclusion of truth**,* **revealed and established in the incarnation and work of redemption!**

I say again, the judgment Paul is referring to here **is *the ultimate conclusion that he came to in the truth of the gospel.***

Where did Paul get that conclusion from?

From dwelling in the truth of God's faithfulness; *in the truth of God's <u>faith</u>*!

I say again: **Paul got his strong faith conclusion from dwelling in the truth of God's <u>Faith</u>, and from dwelling in the truth of God's integrity!**

How do I measure God's integrity?

I can only accurately measure that integrity *by what happened legally when Jesus died on behalf of the human race!*

So Paul says,

*"Let **this** be your mind!"*

*"Let **this ultimate conclusion** be your judgment!"*

Do you see that **it's not an excuse for sin!**

Do you see that this accurate conclusion in the truth of the gospel, ultimate truth, ***causes you to triumph over every attempt of evil to ensnare you!***

Let's look at 1 Corinthians 10:12 & 13 also.

Chapter 4

God Is Faithful!

1 Corinthians 10:12,

*"**Therefore**, let anyone who thinks that he stands, take heed, lest he fall"*

In other words, do not take your standing for granted. Test yourself; examine yourself, *in the light of the truth of the gospel, **in the light of redemption truth**, and then draw from the Christ **within you!***

Don't let your standing in Christ just become another religious doctrine, *another religious principle in your life* ...like going to a church meeting on a Sunday morning,

'Oh, brother Rudi, it's just part of my weekly program, you see' ...*so off I go, and I have to get built up and encouraged all over again, Sunday after Sunday, **because I never seem to grasp it for myself!***

Listen, Paul says, *"STAND ...having done all to stand"* (Ephesians 6:13 & 14)

And then, *"...**No temptation,**"* verse 13, (1 Corinthians 10:13) ...Obviously temptation in this context would be **anything that would challenge your standing.**

Paul says in verse 12, *"**Therefore**, let anyone who stands, **<u>take heed</u>,** lest he fall,"*

How am I going to do it?

How am I now going to **take heed**?

Does that mean that I am going to have to walk around with all kinds of anxieties that I accommodate? Because just now, if I don't watch it, I'm going to trip, and slip up, and fall, because, you know, maybe something is going to tempt me today, and I'm going to be ensnared again, real easily, like the rest of humanity…

Man, that is not what Paul is saying!

Let's read verse 13, he says, *"**NO** TEMPTATION…"*

Does your Bible also say, *"**No**"* there?

*"**NO** TEMPTATION…"*

Does that include ***any size*** temptation ...***any kind*** of temptation ...***any time*** that temptation could come?

Yes, it does, amen?!

Paul says,

*"**No** temptation has overtaken you (or seized you, or ensnared you, or come upon you) **that is not common to all mankind"***

Paul, what are you saying?

How is that going to help me?

How is that going to prevent me from being overtaken or ensnared by the same temptations everybody else gets ensnared with?

You see; if you don't take the time or make the effort to understand correctly what Paul is saying, you can take this scripture and your imagination can run wild with it and you can think, *'Oh well, that means everybody is doing it, so then I can do it as well! I mean, everyone is going to have to fall sooner or later, because Paul said so right here himself,'*

So that becomes our excuse?!

No man, **don't be ridiculous!**

Let's read on, and let's discover together what Paul is really saying there in the rest of verse 13.

Paul says, *"**God is faithful**…"*

In other words, *"Don't look to that which is common to man, look to that which is common with God! **Look to God's faith! And also look to the fact that God is faithful**…"*

Listen, don't try and measure your ability to escape temptation by what is common to Man, by Man's thinking, and Man's willpower, and Man's natural ability,

No, measure your ability by God's faith, and by God's faithfulness to uphold His word, to uphold His truth, *to strengthen and uphold even you!*

God's faith is infallible!

Therefore, God's faithfulness is infallible!

God is unfailing in His faithfulness!

Paul says,

*"**God is faithful,** and He will not let you be tempted beyond your strength…"*

Wait a minute Paul, I thought you said that my strength is measured by that which is common to Man?

No, listen, you have it wrong! The truth is: **Your strength** **is measured** **by God's faith** **concerning you!**

Your strength **is measured** **by God's** **faithfulness!**

Listen, God's faith, and God's faithfulness ***becomes your strength!***

You are not supposed to draw from your own ability to resist temptation!

You are called to draw from the resource of God's faith ...***from the resource of God's strength deposited in you, by that faith; by your understanding of God's truth!***

You are called to draw from that resource of God's strength within you!

He dwells in you, He lives in you; He <u>is</u> **in you! The great I AM is** <u>in</u> **you, *to strengthen you!***

God is faithful!

He watches over His word to perform it; to make it good, *to make it reality!*

He reinforces His truth within you *with power, with DUNAMIS, with Holy Spirit <u>enablement</u>!*

What is that resource of God's strength within me, that I am to draw from?

It's the very faith of God deposited within me!

It's the truth; the reality of *everything that God did in Christ on my behalf, when He raised Him from the dead.*

I was raised with Him to newness of life!

I was raised with Him, and seated with Him in the heavenly realm; *in that unseen realm of spirit reality, in that unseen realm of spirit legality, in that unseen realm of spirit truth and spirit strength and power and authority!*

I was raised with Him, and seated with Him in a place of power and authority!

I was raised to newness of life in Him!

I was raised with Him and seated with Him <u>*far above*</u> *all* principality and power and might and dominion ...*above all evil; above <u>all</u> temptation!*

Hallelujah!

God's ability to keep His word *is His strength!* That's God's faithfulness!

He prophesied hundreds of years, even thousands of years, *before it happened historically.*

He prophesied in Genesis, through Moses, the prophet, and He said, *"The Seed of the women will <u>crush</u> the serpent's head!"*

He prophesied that combat between light and darkness, **which led to the cross,**

But He also said: *"My Son will <u>win</u>!"*

He said through David,

"My soul will not be left in Hades!"

He prophesied the resurrection!

God's own confidence in His own integrity, not *ever* in all of human history, not *ever* in all that time, *was ever shaken!*

John declares in 1 John 5:9,

"Now if it is reasonable for us to be readily persuaded by the evidence that people may lay out before us, **how much more certainty is there in the evidence that God has compellingly borne witness to concerning His Son!"** - Mirror Study Bible

John says in John 1:1, **"To go back to the very beginning is to find the Word already present there; face to face with God"**

This Word then, *translated into the prophetic promise in Scripture, and pointing to the Messiah, the Redeemer, for centuries,* that very LOGOS; **the very LOGOS Himself** finally became flesh and forever divided human history into a BC and AD. (Into a before Christ and after Christ).

Hey, the very heavens declare His glory; night to night exhibits the giant solar testimony that is mathematically precise ...revealing that the Godhead knew before time was, the exact moment they would enter our history as a man, in the person of Jesus Christ, and they also therefore knew, from before time began, the exact moment the Messiah would expire on the cross and be raised again from the dead!

As I said; they declared it in the prophetic word and bore witness to is in the stars; in our very solar system!

A friend of mine stumbled upon this article a while back by Astronomer Phil Plait, and shared it with me. It's about the unique lining up of Venus, Mars, and the Moon, and his conclusion...

"That to me is one of the most profound and wonderful things about viewing the sky: The utter inevitability of the motions of celestial objects; knowing that, with keen enough observations and a grasp of the math, this event could have been predicted millennia ago, and would have occurred right on time!"

Hey, just think about it! It is truly mind boggling! **God is faithful;** He sustains it all by His LOGOS; by the Word of His power – or by the power of His love for us revealed in Jesus Christ! (Hebrews 1:3).

Hey, that enormous unfailing infallible love took on flesh in Jesus!

In Him God revealed that we are indeed the very reason why He upholds the entire universe; it all revolves around His undying immense passionate love for us!

Now wonder David, in meditating upon these things, wrote in Psalm 8:4-8,

"What is man that You, oh Lord, are mindful (or, mind full) of them?! What is the son of man to You that You make so much of him?!"

Hey, **God is faithful, and He is faith full!**

As I said before: **God's own confidence in His own achievement in Christ, and in His own integrity, not** *ever* **in all of human history, not** *ever* **in all that time; in all of time itself,** *was or is ever shaken!*

Neither was or is His love for us!

What took Man captive was Man's own unfaithfulness; *Man's faithlessness.*

So God had to come into an unshakable agreement with Man that would be absolutely sure! …unfailing! …infallible!

60

And God did just that, in Jesus Christ!

Praise God!

"God is faithful, He will not allow you to be tempted beyond your strength,

"…but with the temptation, will also provide the way of escape,

"…so that you may be able to endure it, (or withstand it!)"

Now I believe that within God's provision, there is a place even beyond that *…even beyond enduring it, or having to withstand temptation.*

I believe there is enough provision made in Jesus!

I believe there is a place we can live in beyond temptation!

There is a place in union with Christ we can live in **to where temptation is not something we deal with on a consistent basis,** *or even have to worry about anymore.*

Praise God for the ability to endure temptation!

As we continue to study the Scriptures, we discover that there is a place in the mind of God for the believer, *an abiding place in Him,* **where we are strengthened**, not to keep enduring temptation *and barely overcoming it,* **but to permanently overcome it!**

Do you dare believe that?

Do you dare believe that you can live in such a place of fellowship with God *and of strength, to where it is no longer the believer running away from the devil, but the devil running away from the believer!*

Ha... ha... ha... Hallelujah!

You should go and read James 4:7 for yourself and see what it says. It says,

"Submit yourself to God"

(…submit to His righteousness, to His opinion about your life, submit to His strength that comes from that; embrace His opinion fully, embrace your righteousness, your identity in Him, fully. …So that your ability to resist the devil, *and to overcome him,* is no longer related to anything within yourself, your natural self, your natural identity, *but it's related to God in you!*)

*"**Then**, (out of that place of victory, out of that new found strength)." he says, "…**resist the devil and he will flee from you!**"*

Ha... ha... ha... Hallelujah!

He'll get so confused by your strength, he'll get so confused when you are able to resist him, he'll be so confused, he'll think you're God!

Ha… ha… ha… And in a way he'll be right … ***because it is God, amen!***

Ha… ha… ha… ***Because the very nature of God and the very Spirit of God dwells in*** *your spirit, and His strength is imparted to your spirit!*

Ha... ha... ha... Thank you Holy Spirit!

You see, there is a place that God desires for you to walk in, *where you no longer need to take heed how you walk,* thinking, *'Uh-oh, if I don't watch it, just now I'm going to be snared again,'*

That place God desires for you to walk in is a place where you walk in such confidence, not arrogance, but **confidence** *in the integrity of God's redemption, in the integrity of God's truth, in the integrity of God Himself!*

It's a place of **walking in such confidence** *in the integrity of God's strength within you, because of the faith of God, and because God is faithful!*

There is a place available to the believer ...*it's available to the whole world, to every single individual, amen,* **but only the believer dare walk in it!**

I cannot stress enough that there is such a place available to each and every believer; there is a place God desires for us to walk in, to *live* in, *where we are drawing upon His faith continually, drawing upon His faithfulness, drawing upon our oneness with Him; allowing His faith, and allowing His faithfulness to be my meditation and ongoing conversation;* **to remain my foundation ...the very foundation of my integrity!**

Hallelujah!

That's why Paul says to those guys who are judging him, he says,

'Listen guys, you have a right to judge me, and find out whether I'm really speaking from Christ, but before you get snared and find perhaps something in my life that will give you an excuse, so that you can do wrong,' he says,

"Why don't you rather test the faith for yourself; why don't you rather discover for yourself what is yours in Christ; what is in you already!"

He says,

"Discover for yourself,"

"…then you will also discover where <u>we</u> live from!"

Ha... ha... ha... Hallelujah!

"...You'll discover that same place where we live from for yourself!"

We're not trying to act like mere men; we're not trying to draw from Man's mentality, from what is common to all men, to all mankind.

We are drawing from God's mind, from God's faith, from what is common to God!

God's faith is our energy!

That's our strength!

That's our power!

64

That's our ability!

God's faithfulness is our energy!

Our empowerment!

God's integrity and faithfulness to His word and covenant is our ability!

Ha... ha... ha... Hallelujah! Praise God!

And it is in that light that Paul says,

*"**Now,** I appeal to you, **that you all be <u>of the same mind,</u> (of the same conclusion,) <u>and therefore also</u> of the same judgment"*

Let's not judge by appearances!

Let's not judge by another person's failure!

Or another person's success even!

Let's rather judge ourselves by the word of God; by the "logos" that became flesh, and by the word of Christ; by the work of redemption

…And therefore, let's not continue to give the enemy any further advantage through our ignorance – through us carrying on like mere men; carrying on like common Man; like all other people!

WE ARE NOT MERE MEN!

That's what the Scripture teaches!

WE ARE NOT JUST ORDINARY MEN!

We are ordinary men, in the sense that we don't lean on the fact that we're something in the flesh; *some superhuman or something.*

We are not something in the flesh; *in the flesh, we are nothing; just ordinary men.*

...But God takes us, ordinary men as we are, *and He puts His faith within us, and He Himself is within us, and He puts His extra ordinary within us, and He confounds the wise!*

Chapter 5

Have The Faith Of God!

You know, the secret to the teaching ministry is being able to be a good student, and Paul knew it, he says,

"By this time you yourselves ought to be teachers,"

Why did he say that in the book of Hebrews?

Because he knew it. He knew that by this time they ought to be teachers, because *he knew that **the word produces after its own kind.***

If you continue to have the right attitude, if you keep reading and listening with the utmost attention, *you cannot help but eventually **explode with the faith of God!***

Ha… ha… ha… That's the secret, right there!

If you read or listen with the kind of attitude that says, *'I know it all, oh yeah brother, I've heard it all before, I can tell you a whole bunch of stuff, I even have more revelation than you, brother Rudi,'* Then, I am afraid, my brother, *you'll never really enter into the depths of the secret place of the Most High; **you'll never truly learn the source of life!** You'll never learn or have an ongoing encounter with **what really matters!** You'll never really learn **the**

secret to it all, *…the secret of life more abundantly!*

If you don't learn **to appreciate**, *then you'll never learn anything worth learning!*

*...And you'll never grow **beyond** your past experience!*

One of my African friends once told me something, and I'll never forget it, he told me,

"Brother, if you want to learn something, act foolish!"

Not proper English, *but great wisdom!* Ha… ha… ha…

If you are still with me, I want us to quickly look at Joel Chapter 3,

Joel 3:10,

"Beat your plowshares into swords, and your pruning hooks into spears! Let the weak say, 'I'm a warrior!'"

Let the weak person say,

"I'm a warrior!"

'How can I do that brother Rudi, without being presumptuous, foolish, or just an outright liar?'

*"Let the weak say, '**I'm strong!**'"* says another translation.

Where do I draw strength from *that I do not feel, and that I do not feel I have?*

I mean, where do I draw strength from *that I am not conscious of in my natural ability?*

Where do I draw wisdom from *that I was not educated in?*

Where do I draw ability from *that was not mine by personal achievement?*

"Let the weak say, 'I am strong!'"

I believe **the secret is *in covenant knowledge.***

That strength comes to us as we begin to discover the value, the merit of the kind of integrity that was given us in covenant, through Jesus.

Let's continue to study together now, there in Romans Chapter 4.

You may have read this verse of scripture many times before, or heard it preached just as many times, *but I want you to hear it today in your spirit for what it's really worth, **for what it really says**, amen. Read it and hear it for what it's truly worth in the spirit, **let it mix together with faith in your heart!***

Paul starts off by saying,

"What then shall we say about Abraham, our forefather…?"

Abraham is known as *"the father of us all,"* for he is known as *"the father of faith."*

Romans 4:16 says,

"That is why it depends on faith, in order that the promise may rest on grace and be guaranteed to all his descendants, not only to the adherents of the Law, but also to those who share in the same faith as Abraham, for he is the father of us all,"

Now verse 17 says,

"…just as it is written, "I have made you the father of (the) many nations (all of them)," in the presence of the God in whom he believed, who gives life to the dead and calls into existence the things that do not yet exist."

The Taylor translation says there,

*"…who speaks of future events **with as much certainty** as though they were already past."*

That became the very foundation to Abraham's faith: *God's ability to call into existence the things that do not yet exist; His ability to speak of future events as though they are already past!*

In other words, *it is **God's integrity, God's trustworthiness, God's faith, God's faithfulness** that Abraham put his faith in.*

It became the foundation to Abraham's faith!

…and it strengthened him, and it pleased God,

*...and that faith was reckoned to him for righteousness, **and God's power became his portion!***

And so we read how God says to him,

*'Abraham, your faith is my faith! Embrace **My faith!** I call things into existence that do not yet appear!'*

*And it makes it clear there that Abraham received the testimony of God, **he yielded to it, and embraced it; he believed it and began to expect the things God is calling into existence to come into being!** He embraced what God said, and so it came to be that **Abraham believed God!***

Now let's look at Mark Chapter 11.

Mark 11:22, ***"Have faith in God…"***

But if you are a scholar or a student of the Bible, you will know that in the original text written in the Greek language the writer uses an *objective genitive tense* there in that verse.

And what it means is that this verse shouldn't really read, *"Have faith in,"* but it should rather read, ***"Have <u>the faith of</u>…"***

Now wouldn't you agree that that makes a bit of a difference!

[Read Mark 11:22 in the A.S. Worrel Translation if you must. Jesus' phrase, *"Have faith in God,"* the Greek genitive used there, includes a "genus" or "kind," thus it involves the *"God-kind of faith,"* or, *"The very faith of God Himself"* because God is the very origin of that faith; **faith itself originates in Him.** That's why Jesus actually said: ***"Have the faith of God,"*** and it should be translated that way, instead of the usual, *"Have faith in God"* as

71

most of our regular translations translated it to say, according to A.T. Robertson, who was known as the "granddaddy" of all Greek grammarians when he was alive. His book, *A Grammar of the Greek New Testament in the Light of Historical Research* is considered one of the most advanced in Greek grammars].

But that's getting off track now.

So, Jesus basically said that there is only one faith that matters; there is only **one faith,** (Ephesians 4:5) amen, and that's **the faith of God!**

So, (Mark 11:22), Jesus said, *"**Have the faith of God**"*

In other words, *"…**Agree with His faith;** have the **same** faith* (the **same** conviction and expectation) *as the God who calls those things that be not, as though they were"*

"Have the faith of God!"

And then verse 23 says, *"**Truly, I say** to you…"*

Would you agree with me that that word *"**truly**"* used here by Jesus, would suggest **the faithfulness of God; *the integrity of God?!***

*"**Truly, I say** to you, whoever says to this mountain, 'Be taken up and cast into the sea!' **and do not doubt in his heart, but believe that those things which he says shall come to pass,** he shall have whatever he says!"*

Now you truly have to be in <u>fellowship</u> with God to have His kind of faith and to grasp that kind of authority!

...To even begin to have His kind of faith to speak to anything, amen, not to even mention a mountain!

*"**Truly <u>I</u> say** to you, whoever says to this mountain, 'Be taken up and cast into the sea!' **and do not doubt in his heart**..."*

Now imagine this man that does this. ***This man is acting like God!***

And not just through some principle that he studied; *some principle of **how faith works**, no,* this man is acting like God, and doing these things, *and **he doesn't doubt in his heart**, but he is actually doing these things,* not through some principle that he studied, ***but through deep intimate fellowship that he entertains!***

It's the faith of God that is rubbing off on his spirit!

And that faith gives him a new kind of attitude towards the mountain!

He gains a new attitude towards the impossible!

*…**because God now rubs off on him!***

I mean, just look at what happens to him, *"… **he does not doubt in his heart, <u>but believes that what he says will come to pass</u>!**"*

And then Jesus says,

"Look, it will be done for him!"

"Therefore, I tell you, whatever you ask in prayer (whatever you ask while in **fellowship**) *believing*…"

He says, *"Whatever you ask for, believe..."*

"And what you therefore fully embrace, or believe ...you receive!"

Believing *is receiving,* amen!

He says, *"...it will be yours!"*

Again, that is a scripture for the Greek scholars and students among you to go and read for yourself and to go and look up in your Greek-English Lexicon and your Strong's Concordance, because the word, *"receive"* is the Greek word, ALABETE and that word is only used *in the prophetic perfect tense.*

In many translations it is either translated in the present or future tense, which then reads,

"…believe that you will receive it,"

or it reads,

"…believe that you receive it,"

…Which sounds nice, but really, this scripture sounded so bold, too bold in fact, to almost every one of the translators, and so they were forced to have to tone it down a bit, but what they really ended up doing is changing it and watering it down to mean less than what Jesus meant for it to say.

The *prophetic perfect tense* used in that word, ALABETE **speaks of the certainty of a future event *as though it already happened.***

Now if that is not referring to a person operating in the faith of God, *that same faith of God mentioned in the previous verse,* then I don't know what else it could be referring to.

So the more correct translation of this verse should read:

"…believe that you have received it,"

Listen, we are dealing here with **the infallibility of *God's intention!***

And we are dealing with **the infallibility of *God's truth!***

Hey, God is not going to be swayed by circumstances.

He is absolutely persuaded about your life!

Even if your mountain might appear to you like a monstrous mountain in front of you, **God says, *"You're invincible!"***

Now God holds me, the believer, responsible, *to so fellowship with Him, to so fellowship with His truth, to so fellowship with His faith; to so fellowship with the faith of God, that I can speak the faith of God*!

We can speak the faith of God!

You can speak <u>from out of the faith of God</u> deposited in your spirit!

I can speak <u>forth</u> *the life of God!*

…And release the very <u>energy</u> of God; the very DUNAMIS, the very power of God!

...From within me!

…<u>Grasping and realizing</u> that CHRIST IS WITHIN me!

And therefore, *regardless of my circumstances; regardless of what I may be facing on the outside; regardless of what may be coming against me,* I remain unchallenged in my spirit!

I say again: *I remain unchallenged in my spirit!*

…immovable!

…steadfast!

Ha... ha... ha... Hallelujah!

Praise God!

It is the very faith of God that sustains me; *it sustains my trust in Him!*

He is the one who sustains me by His faith, *which He makes alive within me by the Holy Spirit;* by the Spirit of Truth *as I KAVAH with Him; as I <u>entwine</u> with Him in <u>fellowship</u>!*

Chapter 6

The Glory Within Us!

Hey, separation from God is a lie we believed and lived; *it's an illusion Jesus came to debunk and obliterate!*

It is simply amazing to discover that **God in all His fullness** *dwells in us, and He isn't going anywhere!*

God doesn't dwell in temples made with human hands, *He is way too big for that;* no structure can contain Him, ***but*** *even though the heavens itself cannot contain God, and the earth is but merely His footstool,* yet Ecclesiastes 3:11 declares that **God has placed <u>eternity</u> within the heart of Man;** *within every single one of us!*

Jesus Himself constantly emphasized the fact that the kingdom of God **is at hand** *because it is within you!* - Luke 17:20-21.

Hey, separation is a lie; God isn't going anywhere; *because He is everywhere!* God is larger than life; *He is reality itself!* **He is the very essence of reality! At the very core of everything that is, everything that exists;** *at the core of all matter,* **you will find Him there! He upholds it all and He takes up all the space!**

Hey, eternity dwells within you *right now!*

Eternity is not some delayed happening, in your far or perhaps near future. **Eternity is exactly *right now; this very moment,* we are in eternity!**

Hey, we cannot ever become more eternal than what we already are in this very moment; *we are eternal beings!*

We are inseparably connected to the eternal realm; *to God – for in Him we live and move and have our very being!* - Acts 17:28.

We are just, right now even, embraced in this eternal dance of life, *with the Author of life itself.* He already generously gives to all, life, breath and all other things; *all things exist through Him and for Him,* and **He upholds all things** in His power, in His might, and His glory; **in Him *all things consist,*** all things *are held together* and maintained *in Him!*

All you would but need to do is go look up and study Quantum Entanglement and Quack Theory to discover that at the base of reality there are these sound-waves originating and resonating out from that eternal realm, almost like Jacob's ladder, ha... ha... ha...
connecting the eternal and natural realms together, *for God **upholds all things** by His LOGOS; by the Word proceeding from His power; and by **the very power** of His **Word – by the very power of CHRIST!*** - Hebrews 1:3

So, we are already embraced in this eternal dance of life, with Life and Love Himself!

Ha... ha... ha... Hallelujah! Whether we know it or not; even whether we believe it or not, it doesn't matter, *it is the **very basis of reality** itself!*

So, whether we know it or not, or believe it or not, we already stand invited by God to participate *fully in this realm; in the Christ-realm – in the God-realm!*

We have direct access to the *eternal realm; to the supernatural SHEKINAH GLORY-realm; to the very realm in which **God in all His power and all His glory and all His fullness takes up all the space!***

I am talking about that Spirit-dimension, that eternal Spirit-realm *in which the very presence and person of God saturates the entire place!*

Ha... ha... ha... talk about Quantum Entanglement! It's become reality for those who have discovered their life in the Spirit; *their true identity,* and so, they no longer live their lives merely according to a natural identity, amen!?

Hey, **there is no separation between us and God; between us and that Spirit-dimension! Separation is an illusion, *a convenient lie, a paper-thin wall <u>God wants to break through</u>!***

*God wants us to understand eternity **and connect with eternity! And He wants us to help others connect to it as well!***

We are <u>in</u> eternity, amen!?

God wants us to **AWAKEN to our beingness in Him;** He wants us to simply AWAKEN by the help of the Holy Spirit of Truth **UNVEILING to us that REALITY, that TRUTH;** *that eternal Spirit-dimension, and our INSEPERABLE connection to it!*

You see, the truth the Holy Spirit comes to UNVEIL to us lines up with what has been revealed about us by God in the person of Jesus Christ!

In Him God unveiled ultimate reality! - John 14:20.

In Jesus God revealed our oneness with Him and He revealed that separation is ultimately a lie!

Hey that is *ultimate reality!*

But what I want us to get to is the fact that God wants us to learn **to connect with that supernatural Spirit-realm within us,** *so that we can manifest His GLORY!*

*"For all of creation is crying out for, and waiting with bated breath, **for the full manifestation and revealing of the son's of God for who they are; the very children of God Himself!"*** - Romans 8:19.

Hey, Jesus said, *"The same supernatural works I do, you shall do also, and even greater works than these, you shall do!"* - John 14:12.

Listen, I say again: The incarnation (Jesus), is **the fullness of the oneness between God and man on display!**

He in His person represents a restored relationship!

Thus, what Jesus, as a man representing the eternal union between God and Man, *was able to reveal and manifest* ...I say again: **What Jesus was able to reveal and manifest, He then <u>fully redeemed</u>** ...*FOR US <u>to also now reveal and manifest</u>!*

He said, *"As the Father has sent Me* (to accurately represent and reveal Him for who He really is, as the true Father and Daddy of the human race ...*As the Father has sent Me* to fully manifest His person and His power and His love to people, including healing the sick and performing miracles) *so send I you* (to do the same; to also accurately represent and reveal the Father for who He really is, and to fully manifest His person and His power and His glory and His love to all people; *including healing the sick and performing miracles, **just like I did!***)*" - John 20:21.

Wow! *"As the Father has sent Me, so send I you!"* Let that sink in for a second, before moving on!

Hey, it is high time for us to begin to grasp that that eternal realm we are partakers of; the realm of God, that Spirit-realm where God exists in, **is all around us, and within us,** *but it is a realm which is outside of time and space – **it's of another dimension;** it supersedes this natural dimension.*

The laws and rules of the natural dimension; the Laws of Physics do not apply *to that timeless eternal immortal Spirit-realm!*

When we connect with God, and become <u>**aware**</u> **of our oneness with Him, and simply become** <u>**conscious**</u> **of His most immediate nearness;** *of His very intimate presence,* **we enter the supernatural-realm, the GLORY-realm,** <u>*where everything is possible*</u>*!*

Nothing is impossible to him who enters this realm!

And as we, out of that <u>**conscious awareness**</u> **of Him,** *allow that Spirit-realm, that Glory-realm to begin to flow and manifest out of us,* <u>*supernatural things*</u> *begin to happen!*

In that realm, none of the natural laws, none of the Laws of Physics that govern this natural dimension apply!

In that realm, and from out of that realm axeheads can begin to float! - 2 Kings 6:5-7.

Oh yes, even gravity itself can become temporarily suspended!

How else do you think both Jesus and Peter managed to walk on the water? - Matthew 14:22-33.

We may not understand the science of what had to happen there *to make that possible, **to make that a reality,*** but whatever needed to happen, happened, because it really did happen; **they literally walked on water!**

I know we are getting a little too deep now for some, ha... ha... ha... no pun intended. But I know some people's minds might be getting stretched by this *to the point where it might become a little uncomfortable to them, and quite scary, and just about impossible to believe* ...but hey, it's like old wine skins about to burst, ha... ha... ha... but trust me, *those old whine skins need to bust wide open,* **so a new wineskin, a new frame of reference, a brand new paradigm can be embraced in your thinking and your believing!** So come on, hang in there with me, *"Enlarge the place of your habitation, and let the curtains of your tent be stretched all the way out; let go of the old and hold nothing back, yield yourself fully to the what the Spirit of God wants to do within you, so, lengthen those cords, and strengthen your stakes in it's new position!"* - Isaiah 54:2.

For truly we are seated with Christ in the heavenly places; *in that very realm of Spirit-reality and authority!*

Indeed, *the new boundary lines have truly fallen for us in pleasant places, and **we have a*** *tremendous, delightful, spiritual inheritance!*

We are heirs of God and of that realm in which He abides; *co-heirs with Christ Jesus!*

Consider with me just for a moment the Old Covenant prophetic picture of the Tent of Meeting, or the SKENOS; the Skin Tabernacle in Moses' time, and the Rock of Stone Temple of Kind Solomon's time, with it's inner sanctuary or most holy place, the holy of holies, containing the very *"Ark of the Testimony,"* also known as, *"The Ark of the Covenant."* - Exodus 24:9-31:18; Exodus 33:7-11; 1 Kings 6; Hebrews 9:1-10; 14-15; 23-28.

Paul explained in the New Testament how that Temple was merely a prophetic picture that has come to it's **fullness**, in that, Jesus is the fulfillment of all prophetic imagery hidden throughout the Old Covenant Scriptures and life of Israel, but not only that, He is actually **the fountainhead and conclusion of faith,** meaning that **in Him we discover** that **we now are that inner sanctuary,** *where God dwells in all His fullness!*

Our spirits represent, and in fact <u>are</u> now, the holy of holies, containing the *"Ark of the Covenant,"* **or the** *"Ark of the Testimony"* **which is** *Christ, and His work of redemption!* (1 Corinthians 3:16; 1 Corinthians 6:19; 2 Corinthians 5:1-5; 2 Corinthians 6:16).

That *"Ark of the Covenant;"* that *"Ark of the Testimony"* meaning, ___**Christ**___ **in His person, in His _fullness_, represents** *the abiding GLORY of God!*

In fact, **it is CHRIST IN YOU which is the hope of GLORY!** - Colossians 1:27.

Ha... ha... ha... Hallelujah!

Either way, do you still remember the 3 items inside the Old Covenant *"Ark of the Testimony or Covenant"*?

There was the clay jar or, earthen vessel, containing the Manna (Exodus 16:32-35), **representing the prophetic word that was to become flesh; that true Bread from Heaven**, (Jesus and what He came to share; **His message, His gospel,** *which will never grow old, decay or die.*

Paul said: *"Now we have **this treasure in earthen vessels**"* [2 Corinthians 4:7]

Hey, that LOGOS; that gospel message about Jesus and His work of redemption, *that very treasure we cherish within ourselves* **is the Manna; the very bread of Heaven** *still multiplying and feeding the nations!* It is still being digested by them and becoming a treasure they cherish within their earthen vessels as well!)

Any way, inside that Old Covenant *"Ark of the Covenant or Testimony,"* **representing Christ; _His work of redemption,_** there are 3 items: The clay Jar, or earthen vessel containing the

Manna, and then there are the Stone Tablets (Exodus 16:34) **representing the Law of Moses** *written within our hearts,* or better yet, it represents **the image and likeness of God engraved upon our inner-man;** *that very LOGOS which declares our true identity restored, face to face with God as in a mirror.*

And then the last item within the Ark was the Rod of Aaron (Numbers 17:5-10; Hebrews 9:4), **representing our priestly authority,** *which is the very authority of Jesus, the Good Shepherd.*

Jesus' resurrection, and our innocence confirmed in it, is the very foundation of that authority.

Thus, the Rod of Aaron *represents the Law of the Spirit of Life in Christ Jesus – the Christ-life, as well as His resurrection authority and power, within us!*

What I want you to notice about all that though is that that Old Covenant *"Ark of the Covenant or Testimony"* **represented and to some measure contained, or was filled with, or saturated by, the very GLORY of God;** thus it represented *that eternal Spirit-realm within Christ, but also now revealed to be within us, in which God dwells in all His fullness.*

Through embracing the faith of God revealed in the work of redemption and what was accomplished there, **we now have direct access to that realm,** as indicated by the fact that the veil of separation between the inner sanctuary and outer court was torn from top to bottom! - Matthew 27:50-51.

But what I want us to notice is that *whatever went into that ancient physical "Ark of the Covenant, or the Ark of the Testimony"* **entered that supernatural timeless GLORY realm and dimension, and was physically preserved there in that *"Ark"* and in that realm!**

I love that scripture which says that, *"**The self-same Holy Spirit which raised Christ from the dead lives and dwells and abides in us, and therefore also quickens, or gives life to our mortal bodies.**"* - Romans 8:10-11.

(Our bodies are **mortal,** meaning, they are subject to mortality; they are subject to this natural dimension; they are subject therefore to aging, sickness, death and decay. Our bodies have a definite *"Sell-by, date."*)

...**But the Spirit of Him who raised Christ from the dead, dwells in us,** *and from within us now makes available a constant fresh supply of that same resurrection life,* **which can be applied even to our own mortal bodies,** *as well as the bodies of others,* <u>as a temporary fix</u>**, and a sign and a wonder!**

For instance, even though Jesus healed the sick and even raised Lazarus from the dead, as a spectacular sign and a wonder, *they all eventually died; including Lazarus.*

But what I want you to realize is that in spite of the frailties of the human body and it's limitations, **we are called to manifest God's glory from within us;** *from within our spirit.* **We are called to manifest the very splendor of His person, and of His very power,** *the same way Jesus did.* - Matthew 10:7-8; Mark 16:17-18.

That's why I also love what Acts 10:38 reveals about Jesus, *and by implication,* **_about us_** *as well!*

It says that,

*"**God anointed <u>the man</u>, Jesus Christ of Nazareth, with the Holy Spirit and His power, and thus, he went about doing good and healing all who were oppressed of the Devil, <u>for God was with Him</u>!**"*

But let's get back to the prophetic image of the *"Ark of the Covenant or, Ark of the Testimony"* and its hidden messages I am trying to explain.

Now, the Manna that fell in the desert, was supposed to be gathered and eaten every single morning, or it would be melted away by the afternoon, when the sun grew hot. - Exodus 16:21. It could not be saved for tomorrow, for it would begin to stink and get maggots in it, and thus it represented the fact that **we live in a fresh <u>right now</u> reality;** *faith is a constant fresh <u>right now reality</u>,* **sustained by the KHOL or KALAL LOGOS made flesh; by the Word** *in it's most complete context!* (Romans 1:17; Luke 4:4.)

But listen now, it was only on the Sabbath day that the Manna was preserved from the previous day, *but only as long as it was still the Sabbath!* - Exodus 16:23-26 & 30.

The Sabbath represents **us entering into the rest of God *through faith,*** wherein *we cease from all our labors,* but instead, **we celebrate our oneness with Him.**

In other words, **that celebration of our oneness with Him *becomes an environment in which He sustains us, and becomes our very life!***

So, I want you to notice that the Manna that would otherwise decay **did not decay** *in the Sabbath day.* **It was preserved in immortality,** *at least while it entered the Sabbath day!*

Hey, our spirits have entered that realm and that state, permanently, *as we celebrate Him in us, and us in Him!*

But from a natural standpoint I want you to notice that **even the natural phenomenon of decay is suspended *by the introduction and intervention of the supernatural realm into the realm of the natural.***

Now I want you to notice though that once the Manna entered the *"Ark of the Covenant, or Testimony"* decay was suspended indefinitely; **it was fully preserved in the timeless eternal immortal GLORY-realm or Spirit-dimension.**

The natural rules no longer applied, in other words, what could be considered as reality itself, was no longer reality; the very Laws of Physics that uphold this natural dimension, was suspended; thus a different reality applied – the ultimate reality!

That Spirit-dimension reality is greater than this natural-reality dimension we live our lives in.

That's why Paul said, *"We live by faith, and not by sight!"* - 2 Corinthians 5:7-9.

Now I want you to notice as well that the same thing that happened to the Manna, also happened with the Shepherd's Staff or, Rod of Aaron. It was made of an almond tree branch, and in the *"Ark of the Covenant, or Testimony" even though it had no roots, and no water, or even dirt to grow in; and even though there was no sunlight either,* yet the almond branch came alive and was sustained in timeless immortality, complete with almond blossoms ...*even bearing fruit and producing almonds.* (Numbers 17:6-11).

It is interesting to note that the almond tree is the first to blossom in the spring **and thus it represents both resurrection life and the fact that just like Jesus, we are God's first fruits that belong to Him exclusively *and we prophetically represent to God, the entire harvest manifesting in it's fullness.* - John 12:24; 1 Peter 1:10-11.

That GLORY-realm, that supper-natural Spirit-realm, that realm of Divine power and resurrection life and immortality *is within us and available to us to access!*

Jesus brought that realm to light through the gospel. - 2 Timothy 1:10.

Both Peter and Paul and also the rest of the apostles and many of the saints in the early church **began to grasp that it is available for us to walk in, in the now, *and almost all of them began to access it.***

Hey, it is recorded for us and written about in many places in the book of Acts; you can go read it for yourself there.

I love what Peter said to the lame man at the Gate Beautiful, he said, *"**Such as I have, give I unto you!** In the Name of Jesus rise up and walk. And he took the man by the right hand and helped him up, and **instantly the man's feet and ankles became strong,** and so, he jumped to His feet and began to walk. Then he went with them into the temple courts and he was walking and leaping, even jumping, and praising God!"* Acts 3:6-8.

Jesus talked about how this works, *this supernatural, faith-realm,* when He said,

*"Do you not say; 'There is **4 more long months,** and **only then** comes the harvest?' **But** I say unto you, lift up your heads, and open your eyes; look, **the fields are already white unto harvest!"** -* John 4:35.

Ha... ha... ha... This reminds me of the prophetic word in Amos 9:13-15,

"The days are coming, declares the Lord, ***when the reaper will overtake the plowman, and the planter, by the one treading grapes.*** *New wine will drip from the mountains and flow from all the hills, and I will bring my people back from their exile. They will rebuild the ruined cities and live in them. They will plant vineyards and drink their wine; they will make gardens and eat their fruit! I will firmly plant my people in their own Land, never again to be uprooted from that place I have given them to dwell in," says the Lord your God"*

Oh, hallelujah! I love it!

Time is suspended and it's natural process canceled ***in that supernatural GLORY-realm!***

That means, before the plowman even has time to plow, *the harvest will* **suddenly manifest** *and the reaper will have to overtake and take the place of the plowman!*

It sound to me like something else Jesus said; He said:

"I sent you to reap what you have not worked for, others may try to work for it, but you won't have to, you'll just step right in and reap, based on other's labors." - John 4:38.

Ha... ha... ha... (Hey, the prophets of old labored, they diligently searched out and prophetically proclaimed these things in
92

advance, and then the Godhead labored on our behalf as well, to bring it all into reality!

*"...**I sent you <u>to reap what you have not worked for</u>!**"* - John 4:38.)

Right before that, Jesus spoke about that work of redemption in which He would and did restore **unto us** *to that life lived in **oneness** with God; in that supernatural Spirit-and-glory dimension.*

He told them plainly, *"My food is to fulfill the desire of Him who commissioned Me **and to leave no detail of it undone!**"* - John 4:34.

Amos prophesied, (in that previous Scripture I already quoted: Amos 9:13-15) how the planter of grape seeds **will be overtaken and replaced by the one treading out grapes,** *because the laborious natural process and waiting game will be canceled!*

Oh, I love the **suddenlies** of God! And I love the fact that **faith is always now!** All because **the Word is near you**, *in your heart, and in your mouth!* - Romans 10:8 and 10:17, also Hebrews 11:1.

Talking about the treading of grapes and the New Wine being produced, **I love the way Jesus demonstrated** *just how that supernatural dimension of the New Testament and of the indwelling Holy Spirit and His power work,* when He turned the water into wine.

...And many times after that also, when He healed the man born blind, or the man at the pool of Bethesda, etc., etc.

...Or when He multiplied the little boy's lunch and fed the multitudes with only 2 fishes and 5 small loaves of bread, **supernaturally canceling the time it would take to go and catch fish and prepare them,** *even cook them.*

(Because according to Genesis 9:4 and Deuteronomy 12:16, you know, the Jewish customary kosher laws, the Jews did not eat raw fish, remember!)

Jesus also supernaturally, unexplainably so, **canceled the time it would take to sow the seed, grow the harvest, reap the harvest, make bread,** *and bake it,* ha... ha... ha...

What a miracle! What a demonstration **of the GLORY of God and of that supernatural POWER-realm** *we have access to!*

Let's just read how the Mirror Study Bible describes that event in which Jesus *turned the water into wine.*

So much is being unveiled in that scripture passage regarding what God is saying to us, and want us to grasp, concerning the New Covenant, and concerning our life in Christ, i.e. the Christ-life in us, and that supernatural power-and-glory dimension and Spirit-realm within us, *which we have access to.*

Let's just start reading there in John 2:1.

2:1 There was a wedding in Cana, a village in Galilee, which Jesus' mother attended.

2:2 Jesus and his followers were also invited.

2:3 When Mary learned that they had run out of wine, she informed Jesus.

2:4 He responded with, "Well, Ma'am, that's their problem – or do you want me to steal the show here at somebody else's wedding, when my hour of fulfilling my mission has not yet come?"

The footnote reads: *(Religion has run out of wine – Jesus lived aware of his mission, which was to redeem, and restore, [or ignite] the joyous celebration of the union and Romance of the ages – marrying mankind and Divinity! While he is the true joy and wine of the party, he fully understood what it would cost him to drink the cup of mankind's injustice and violence on the cross! See John 12:27, "Now is my soul troubled. And what shall I say? 'Father, save me from this hour'? No, most certainly not, for this very purpose I have come to this hour.)*

2:5 Mary proceeded to line up the waiters to assist Jesus, "Do whatever he tells you to!"

2:6 Now there were six empty stone water pots, used for the ceremonial cleansing of the Jews. They could hold approximately twenty gallons each.

2:7 Jesus asked the waiters to fill these stone jars with water, to the brim.

In the footnote it says: *(Nothing would be left untouched by the effect of the incarnation and the incarnate Word impacting human life entirely – every nook and cranny – spirit, soul, and body! See mirror notes to John 1:51; also 1 John 5:18.)*

2:8 And then when it was done and their task was complete he instructed them to immediately draw from the containers and present it to the governor of the feast; which they did, without hesitation.

2:9 The host of the event tasted the water that has now <u>all of a sudden</u> become wine, but had no clue as to its vintage or origin. The servants didn't tell him a word, so he called the bridegroom.

2:10 "Why would you keep the best wine for last?" Everybody serves the better wine first, so that by the time the cheaper wine is served, no one can tell the difference – and here you surprise us all by bringing this excellent wine from your storehouse. Even though we already had much to drink, it is impossible not to tell its superiority!

I love the footnote there, it says, *(Even minds and spirits intoxicated with inferior religious influences and jargon, can immediately tell the difference, between that which is fake and that which is authentic and real, when the Holy Spirit transforms ordinary human conversation into the wonderful, blissful wine of revelation and spirit-impact that brings forth and produce the miracle of a genuine merry celebration of life!)*

2:11 In this first of the signs and wonders Jesus performed, revealing his 1glory and the glory of God, at a wedding in Cana of Galilee, he gave everyone a foretaste of the beauty, intention, and glory of his mission. And thus, his disciples believed in him.

Footnote: *(The word, DOXA often translated as* **glory,** *comes from the root word, DOKEO, meaning, to form an opinion, a view, an idea or intention, based on real original authentic value and worth. The Hebrew word for* **glory** *is the word KAVOD or KABHODH, meaning important, weight, deference, or heaviness, but primarily it also means, respect, honor, majesty. It speaks of the weight of God's person, of His very presence, and of His opinion, and the enormous power behind it.*

You see, ideas become our eyes – the way we see things. - Dr. C. Baxter Kruger.

Now, if Jesus, by the glory of God, by manifesting that glory, could do this to water – imagine how he can transform ordinary routine days into the invigorating adventure of living the life of our design to the max!

His first miraculous sign was a change within a vessel! A jar of stone. External washing has been upgraded to internal transformation of inner thought processes, and an elevation of the spirit-man to find itself in that supernatural Spirit-realm, experiencing oneness with the Godhead!

Even the angelic realm, or ministering spirits of God, becomes real, and their supernatural ministry and impartation is included as part of the package! - John 1:51.

Hey, that's what you would call: Completely transformed to the "brim!"

...And, it wasn't even clean drinking water, but "the kind used for ceremonial washing!"

Meaning, there is nothing Jesus intended to leave out of this transformation.

...And, although it wasn't time for Jesus to give his wine that night at Cana. I believe it was no accident that it was the first miracle – Could there have been a more profound picture of his ministry, and of what his New Wine would do in the lives of ordinary vessels? He thus **revealed his GLORY, and our glory!** *- E. Meaney.*

*"***"They have no wine."** *That's all Mary says to Jesus, after noticing the newlyweds' embarrassment. Could she be more indirect? Yet, he knows what she really wants, and he's not feeling ready, just like when he was sitting exhausted there at Jacob's Well in Samaria, when the Samaritan women approached.*

So, Jesus tells Mary that it's not the right time, the convenient time, for him to reveal both his glory and God's glory, and suffer the
98

consequences. The wine he could make would be free to the guests, but cost him plenty. Mary marches right over to the serving table as if he'd said, "No problem, Mom!" instead of, "No way, Mom!"

She once said a costly yes herself; that's why she's not about to take a "no" for an answer from him.

*But, she was acting under the inspiration of God's Spirit, **because they had no wine.** It suddenly becomes the entire human history she's talking about; life's disappointed guests milling around with empty glasses, from time immemorial.*

Apparently the Holy Spirit speaking from within her has waited long enough for the mighty to fall, for the poor to dance at the wedding, for the kingdom elixir to flow.

The Persian potentates with their three gifts once bent their knees to him. Why is he still constructing cabinets in Nazareth? Mary, and the Holy Spirit wants him out of the house!

So, Jesus had no choice but to give in and thus he produces liquid heaven in preposterous quantities. He and the God in him squanders it on us, the supposed undeserving [according to religion,] who can't even distinguish for ourselves rotgut from Rothschild. He becomes the very wastrel we need him to be. – Thank you, Mary, and thank you Holy Spirit!"

*Here's a prayer for you: "When we are reluctant to act on our Devine Calling from above, Oh God, send the Holy Spirit via the Mary's of our day, to remind us that, "**They have no wine.**" Get us out of the house!" - M. Luti.*

The footnote to John 1:51 states: (*In him [meaning Jesus, the Christ] every definition of separation and distance is canceled!*

Isaiah 55:10-11, "For as the rain and the snow come down from heaven, and return not there without first fulfilling its mission of saturating the earth [all flesh], so shall my Word be that goes forth from my mouth; it shall not return to me empty handed, but it shall accomplish that which I purposed, and it shall prosper in the very thing for which I sent it!"

The prophetic word was destined to become flesh; every nook and cranny of human life is saturated in the incarnation!

Ephesians 1:3 says, "Let's celebrate God! He lavished every blessing heaven has upon us in Christ!"

Ephesians 2:6 continues; "We are co-elevated in his ascension to be equally welcome in the throne room of the heavenly realm, where we are indeed co-seated together with him in his authority."

Ephesians 4:10 makes it plain, "He [this Jesus and His work of redemption] now occupies the ultimate rank of authority, no matter where you may go in any realm or dimension; from the lowest regions [or realm of reality] where he stooped down to, to rescue us, from all the way down there, ascending all the way up to the ultimate reality realm [or region,] even to the highest ranked authority in the heavenly realm [the ultimate realm of reality; the supernatural Spirit-realm of glory and power and majesty,] having flawlessly executed his mission to the full."

Fallen mankind is thus now fully restored to the authority of the authentic life of their true design.

"Jesus has united heaven and earth, the life of God and human life in himself. Just as it was planned before the time of the ages" - Dr. C. Baxter Kruger.)

1 John 5:18 in the Mirror Study Bible says, among other things,

5:18 ...To 1see one's true revealed and now redeemed genesis in God, is to treasure the person you really are by his divine engineering and to remain 4unstained in your thoughts by 3the "I-am-not Tree-system." Those misguided 3ideas that I am not the expression of God on the earth; his image, his likeness on display, can no longer 4attach itself to my thoughts, neither do I allow it to ignite its 2destructive cycle of false humility and religious self-righteousness pride, or its unbelief and depression! Engaging again in those

misguided belief systems and ideas will leave one powerless and helpless! All the systems of this world is based on an ingrained mentality of separation, which in turn is marked by its own unnecessary [3]hardships, labors, annoyances, unmet expectations and frustration! That unbelief and fully embraced lie becomes an all consuming and most exhausting lifestyle of having to prove oneself in every relationship, in a futile striving again for a recognition already yours. That kind of an empty works-oriented pursuit inevitably results in [2]disappointment, condemnation, and rejection, and in the end, all one is left with is pretense (with no real power).

The footnote reads: *(John begins the 3 sentences in verse 18, 19, & 20 with the verb, OIDAMEN, which is the Perfect Active tense of [1]EIDO, **to see**, to observe, to pay attention, to perceive, to know as an eye-witness.*

*The Perfect Indicative Active tense **denotes an action which is perfected or completed in the past, but the effects of which are regarded as continuing into the present, powerfully influencing and shaping it.***

A distorted image of oneself** is what the word, [2]HAMATIA suggests. It comes from, HA, **which is a negative,** and MEROS, which means, **portion or form;** thus, HAMARTIA suggests **being without or outside of one's true allotted form.

The word ₃PONEROS, often translated as **evil,** refers to **the tree of the knowledge of good and evil** [PONEROS] which is full of the fruit of a lost fellowship, identity, value, and innocence. Through hardships, labors, toil and annoyances mankind has striven for generations, in vain, to redeem themselves from their own inaccurate inferior judgments, and their illusions of separation from God, and from that Spirit-dimension He exists in. This only conclude in a spiritual judgment based on performance. Which is the exact opposite to an embraced opinion of approval based on inherent value and worth! The word, ₄HAPTOMAI means, **to fasten itself to, or to cling to something;** it comes from HAPTO meaning, **to kindle a fire; to ignite.**

If there is indeed then nothing wrong with mankind's design, or redemption, there can only be one problem: We are all thinking wrong; **we are thinking inferior thoughts!**

See Isaiah 55:8-9; "Your thoughts are not my thoughts, therefore your ways are not my ways!"

Also, Jeremiah 29:11, "For I intimately know the thoughts I think towards you," says the Lord, "It is thoughts of peace, and not evil, **to give you** a real future, and a living hope in the now."

Isaiah 55:9-10, "Just like the rain and the snow bridges the distance and the gap between heaven and earth, and completely cancels the *drought, so shall my word be; it shall indeed cancel all distance, and every drought condition, and it shall saturate the earth [flesh] with my very presence; my very love and power and glory; every nook and cranny of human life shall again be glorified and filled with glory – in the incarnation of my Spirit-Word: the Incarnation!*

The word indeed became flesh and now indwells us!

For those who can embrace it as ultimate truth, as ultimate reality; in the death and resurrection of Jesus Christ, God has brought final closure to the rule of the "I-am-not Tree system."

The idea of God's absence as well as every definition of distance and separation was canceled for good!

Jesus is God's mind made up about this!

Jesus is God's mind made up about us; about our authority!

Jesus is God's mind made up about the whole human race and what belongs to them!

They are legal heirs of His glory! We are all legal heirs of the glory fully restored!

God is not more Emmanuel to the Jew than what he is to the Gentile.

See John 1:14 which says,

"Suddenly the invisible eternal Word, that invisible eternal reality declared, takes on visible form – the Incarnation! And that incarnation is on full display in human form; in human life, as in a mirror! In him [in Jesus Christ], and now confirmed in us! The most accurate tangible display of God's glory and of God's eternal thought, finds full expression in human life! The eternal Word became a human being; we are his very address; he resides in us! He indeed now captivates our gaze! The very glory of God we see there, is not a religious replica; some kind of religious fake glory; no, he is the authentic begotten Son; our very blueprint! The original glory [that we lost in Adam,] now returns in full! In fact, more than that, God's own glory now is our very inheritance; our portion! Hey, only grace can communicate truth; that ultimate reality, in such complete context!")

Hebrews 1:3 in the Mirror Study Bible says,

1:3 Jesus is indeed the creshendo of God's conversation; he gives complete context and content to the authentic thought, and the life of the ages, meant for us. Everything that God had in mind for mankind is clearly articulated and voiced in him. Jesus is God's Spirit-language, and His language of love! He is the radiant and flawless expression of God's person and glory, as well as his intent for our lives! He mirrors God's character and exhibits His every attribute in human form. He is the voice of God, announcing our redeemed

innocence, and restoration to glory. This voice is the very dynamic that sustains the entire cosmos. He is the force of the universe upholding everything that exists, as the very executive authority of God Himself, enthroned in the boundless measure of his majesty.

The footnote there: *("Having accomplished complete purification of sin and it's influence, he sat down..." His throne is proof of mankind's redeemed innocence and glory!)*

John says, in John 3:16,

3:16 The entire cosmos is the object of God's affection! And he is not about to abandon his creation – the gift of his son is for humanity to realize and enjoy as real, their origin in him who mirrors their authentic birth – begotten not of flesh but of the Father! In this persuasion the life of the ages echoes within the individual and announces loud and clear that the days of regret and sense of inner-loneliness and powerless lost-ness are over!

Let's also read, Romans 5:15-20,

5:15 The only similarity in the comparison between the crash-landing and the gift of God, is that both Adam and Christ represent the masses. However, the grace gift lavished upon mankind in the one man, Jesus Christ supersedes the effect of Adam's failure by far, and is beyond

106

comparison in significance to the idea of death and separation.

5:16 The principle of the gift speaks indeed a different language and brings a radically different equation to the table.

5:17 Death no longer has the final say. Life rules! If the effect of one man's crash-landing engaged mankind in a death-dominated struggle in life, and in their lifestyle, how much more advantaged and advanced is the very same mankind now that they are the recipients of the boundless reservoirs of grace, empowering them to enjoy the dominion of life through the gift of righteousness, all because of that one man, Jesus Christ. Grace is indeed out of all proportion in superiority to the transgression and it's influence.

Then we also read in the footnote: *(Of course none of this takes faith out of the equation! On the contrary, it emphasizes our need to engage with the faith of God! Grace explained and revealed gives context to faith! The very content of the work of redemption, through the incarnation, gives context to faith! Thus, according to Romans 5:1-2 Faith is not what you must do, in order to; no, it's what happens to you because of; it's the very source of Divine power; of the power and glory of God operating both in you and through you!)*

5:21 Just as the idea of death and separation gave sin its platform and power-base to reign from; now grace has taken the initiative and taken over the sovereignty through righteousness revealed, in order to introduce unthreatened life, under the Lordship of Jesus Christ and the truth of his work of redemption over us!

Chapter 7

See Yourself The Way God Sees You!

Having said all that, which is powerful, but a mouthful, I want us to finish off in Genesis Chapter 17 to further unpack this.

I am sure that if you went to Sunday school while growing up, you will remember how God entered into a covenant with a man named Abram, and how Abram had a name change and became Abraham, *because of God's covenant relationship and promise to him.*

His original name, Abram, means: **An exalted father.**

Wow, what a name!

...And what an embarrassment to this man!

His very name was an embarrassment!

I mean, you can just imagine this man traveling and meeting some great princes and great kings along the way, *and they would say,*

'And what is your name?'

And he'd say, *'Abram,'* and they would respond,

'Well, sir, that's a very positive name that your father gave you; an exalted father! Wow, you must have many children then; where are they, can we meet them?'

And then he would have to hang his head low and say, *'Sorry, I have none.'*

If he could, he probably would have wanted to change his own name.

I mean, *'God you expect so much of me, I mean, can't you give me a more comfortable job, you know, I always wanted to be a part of God's plan, but I just want to hide in the background you know, I really don't want to be very prominent God'*

So God says,

*'Okay, I'll change your name, I'll make it even bolder, I'll make it, **Abraham!**'*

Abraham means: **The father of many nations, or, the father of all the nations, of the entire world!**

Ha… ha… ha…

Hallelujah!

You see, God by this time *had already spoken into Abram's heart, but God desired for that word to mix together with faith, so that that word will not fail Abram.*

And so, in order to do that, God began to deal with Abram's <u>identity</u>.

Abram had to <u>realize</u> that God saw him as *Abraham!*

He had to start <u>seeing</u> himself as *Abraham!*

It's not enough for God to see him as Abraham; *he had to start seeing himself that way!*

He had to start seeing himself as Abraham!

God basically said to him,

'Listen Abram, <u>realize</u> what you are in Me! Begin to <u>speak to yourself</u> in terms of My plan for your life! Begin to <u>see yourself</u> and <u>call yourself</u> Abraham! Begin to <u>see</u> yourself <u>in the light of My word</u>!'

'YOU ARE ABRAHAM!'

I mean, can you just imagine, here is this man, he had to live almost all of his life with a name that he didn't really prove, maybe even approved of, *and now he's got to go and reintroduce himself to all his friends!*

'...Ahem, you know that name that I was rather embarrassed about, well, God has given me permission to change it.'

'Oh yes, I remember, so what is it now?'

'Abraham'

'What! What the heck man? You're crazy!'

Ha… ha… ha…

And then the process started of reeducating everyone; and so you know, initially everyone would start speaking to him and say, *'Abram,'* and he would have to interrupt them and say,

'Ahem, let me interrupt you right there, listen man, I've told you before, not Abram, **Abraham!'**

Can you just imagine how often he had to repeat it.

...And repeat it, and repeat it, and repeat it, and repeat it, and repeat it some more!

...And he began to sound like God, in his language and in his confession, because he refused to have any other testimony about himself than the testimony of God!

Paul says in Romans 4 that this man Abraham **came to a place of *unwavering confidence, fully established in his faith!***

He was *fully persuaded* that the God who calls substance out of nothing *is faithful and can be fully relied upon and trusted,* and that His word *is* reality. His word is of greater reality and consequence than anything in existence; *than any other reality!*

He was fully convinced and persuaded *that God watches over His word,* and that God upholds it *and enforces it!*

…That He makes it *reality!*

…**Because He is** *reality itself; the very definition of reality!*

Abraham would no longer be swayed by his past, or by experience, *or by anything in the natural!*

You see, even though he was already an old man in the natural, that which was common to Man in the natural *was not going to be common to him!*

He understood and grasped that He was in covenant with *an uncommon God!*

He said to himself, *"Hey listen you,* **'I am in covenant with a God** <u>that releases His ability to do</u> **through His promise!'**

…And so he began to fully identify himself with that word!

You see, **quite often we fail to experience the word,** *because the word is not mixed in together with faith in our spirit!*

That means, *it has* <u>not yet</u> *become part of our* <u>identity</u> *…because we* <u>do not let it</u> *become part of our identity; we shelve it, in preference of an identity of inferiority!*

So, instead of embracing it, we feel ourselves unworthy, and we choose not to believe it, and we put it on a shelf!

'Yes brother, it's a lovely promise, but there it is, you know, I'll just leave it out there, as lovely sounding words; an **unbelievable** *lovely*

sounding promise' …**And so, there's a distance that remains between you and that word.**

Listen, God says, "Get that word, embrace it fully, make it a part of you, as much a part of you as your name! Come on, comprehend and grasp that word as one with you, as much a part of you as your name, that is, if you even want the secret to God's purpose fulfilled in your life!"

Otherwise, you are just going to be another one of those who say, *'Well, God is unfaithful; His word is unreliable. It doesn't work, because it didn't work for me!'*

Listen, I say again: Get that word into your name; into your personal identity, and begin to identify yourself fully with God's plan for your life!

And do you know what was the next thing that happened in Abraham's life, when he did this; **when he fully embraced what God said?**

You see, God had to then change Abraham's mentality towards his wife, *and He gave her a new name too!*

Her name was **Sarai**, which means: **Yahweh is a prince!**

God changed it to: **Sarah**, which means: *I'm a princess!*

You know it sounds so nice to say:

'Well, praise God, my faith is in God!'

But you know what, *better yet:* **God's faith is in you!**

God's faith is in His workmanship in you!

...**And in His working in you, *through His word, to bring you fully into your destiny as child of God!***

You know, often we can sound so very religious in our worship and our confession of *how able God is,* **but it's remote!**

God wants that truth *near you, lodged deep within your heart!*

God says, <u>YOU</u> ARE A PRINCESS!

But here we are, 'O God, you're my Prince, and you're wonderful, God, I'm in love with you, you're my Prince, I know you've got a great plan for my life!'

…and after a while **it gets rather old now to believe in that plan!**

She still believed that something was going to come out of her, **but nothing happened, until God became real and He changes <u>her</u> name!**

*…***And God does this whole thing; but He did it though Abraham!**

Just in case you don't believe me, let's read it there in Genesis.

Genesis 17:15,

*"And God said to Abraham, 'As regards to Sarai your wife, **you shall not call her name Sarai, but Sarah shall be her name!'"***

*"**You shall call it**…"*

In other words,

*"**Abraham, change your attitude towards your wife!**"*

That's a good word for some husbands! Ha… ha… ha…

He says, *"**Call your wife what I call her!**"*

Hey, **God says,** *'Don't get all legalistic and traditional and religious with your wife's identity **anymore**' …Saying, 'Yahweh alone is a prince,'*

*'**No,**'* He says,

*'**Call her** princess**!**'*

*'**CALL** HER **PRINCESS!**'*

*'**SHE** IS **A PRINCESS!**'*

Husbands call your wives: **Princess!**

Princess Carmen …**you** are a princess!

…You are **my** *PRINCESS!*

Come on now, do it, put your wife's name in there!

Listen, I want you to know that God has in mind for your life, **His focus** …and His purpose, *and nothing less!*

And so you see, God has to introduce His purpose *on the legality of His own integrity!*

That's His focus!

The legality of His own integrity; the legality of what He says, of what He reveals in Christ Jesus, in that work of redemption, *that's His focus!*

And God introduces His purpose based on that legality; *based on the legality of His own integrity!*

Otherwise, my friend, guaranteed, you'll fall; you'll fail!

And then we'll be yet another generation of people that failed God!

But as we determine *to have this mind within us, to have the same mind, the same judgment,* **we become united in the same purpose.**

…And because **we measure ourselves, not by ourselves, but by the word,** we are saying,

'God, **Your intention, Your word, will prosper concerning me! Because I'm going to take Your word into my bosom. I'm going to allow Your word to change even my personality if necessary!**

God, let Your word become the new life within me, the new creation within me, that my life is founded upon. I will not merely be measured by my natural talent, or by my natural attributes, but I'll be measured by who You are!'

"...Let the weak say: 'I am strong!'"

"...beat your plowshares into spears, and your pruning hooks into shields!"

In this book, God says *to you,*

"Change your attitude about your life; YOU are part of My strategy for this earth!"

Listen, *YOU are part of His strategy!*

YOU are part of His purpose!

YOU are part of His plan with the nations!

Hallelujah!

Let us just quickly go to one more Scripture.

Romans 8:5

*"For those who live according to the flesh **set their minds upon the things of the flesh**, but those who live according to the spirit, **set their minds upon the things of the spirit**"*

Who is responsible for where your mind is set?

I'm responsible; you're responsible, amen!

We are responsible *to set our mind upon the things of the spirit!*

That means *I am setting my mind to think **in terms of God's opinion**, in terms of God's word over my life, **in terms of what God has to say in Christ, concerning me!***

…and I know God's word will not fail Him, **therefore, I will not fail Him,** *amen!*

Praise the Lord!

So don't be timid any more, but be bold about *who you are in Christ!*

For God has not given us a spirit of fear; *a spirit of timidity* …but He has given unto us in Christ, **a bold, bold spirit; *a spirit of love, a spirit of power, of empowerment and enablement and a sound mind!***

Hallelujah! They all go hand in hand!

Thank you Father!

I want you to realize that the Holy Spirit is encouraging us *to realize that **there must come a determination in our spirits, a determined adamant mind and attitude, an absolute passionate,** to take a hold of this word, to lay hold of **His word in Christ,** to lay hold of **the truth** of what **really happened** in that work of redemption, **how we have been reconciled and made one with God in the spirit, how we have had the right restored to us to be children of God.***

We must take a hold of this word with a determined spirit, and be adamant about it!

119

Hey, it's not just going to just float into your spirit, and neither are you going to just float into that image portrayed there about you in that word!

It's not simply going to happen; it will never become yours, unless you really grab hold of it, and say, 'I am going to make it mine!'

And God is saying to us,

He wants us, *as much as we want this image for ourselves* ...He wants us *to hold this image before one another!*

Refuse to look at your brother and sister, your friends or your neighbor, in the flesh, *but you determine in your heart to see them in Christ Jesus!*

...To see their true identity in Him!

...To see them standing in the full measure of the stature of Christ; standing strong, in Christ Jesus!

Determine in your heart to SEE them!

...To see them, in Christ Jesus!

Determine in your heart not to see them <u>in the flesh</u>!

...Don't see them, merely IN THE FLESH!

They too are spirit-beings; *God's children, blind and ignorant perhaps, trapped in their sin,* **but God's children none the less!**

Listen, refuse any other impression in your mind about yourself, *or about them!*

Hey, we are all God's children, we are all spirit-beings, *and what God did and accomplished in Christ Jesus applies to us all!* So, I say again: **Refuse any other impression in your mind about yourself, *or about them!***

So, maybe they failed you yesterday, or maybe they failed you this morning even, but what of it; *I don't care how many times they fail you,* **you have the mind and the love and the life of God inside of you that is invincible, amen!**

Listen the enemy would certainly want to nullify the effect of the word in our hearts!

He would come and he would try and throw anything at you and introduce and take advantage of any situation that would cancel the effect of the word, *so that the word will not benefit us.*

…**And the way he often does it is through judgment in our heart towards another, *where we become critical in our hearts and suspicious towards one another.***

But God says very clearly to us through Paul,

"*Let us examine ourselves, to see whether we are holding to the faith* (Holding on to the truth of the word, preferring it over whatever is trying to challenge its authority, its truth and its reality!)"

You see, as we discover Christ within us, then we have a better judgment of the other person …and we realize, hey listen, they too have the image of Christ within them; they too have been made in His image and likeness, and they too have the expression of the Christ-life as a capacity within them, it's within them; *it's within their reach!*

You see, we realize, *'You too have Christ in you'* …and we can do nothing, not me, not you, none of us can do *anything* against the truth; *only for the truth!*

So let's fellowship with the truth and around the truth in our fellowship with one another.

Let's fellowship the truth, amen!

Hallelujah!

Thank you Father!

Father, sometimes we are so timid to respond to You, to respond in faith, *but I thank you that we are no longer common men!*

I thank you for the *strength* of Jesus within us, which makes us a peculiar people, *an uncommon people.*

…And Father, though in the natural it might appear at times that we're shrinking, and losing ground, because things don't seem to work out as we'd like it to work out, but I thank you that **we need not be sidetracked by any appearance; we need not focus on anything**

other than the appearance of the reflection of Your glory in Your word upon our spirits!

So we determine as a covenant people *to walk* in intimate covenant-fellowship with God!

In Jesus Name, amen!

In closing, I urge you to get yourself a copy of the Mirror Study Bible. It is the best paraphrase translation of the Scriptures from the original Greek that I have ever read, and it's available online at Barnes & Noble and several other book sellers.

If you want me or someone a part of our team to come to where you are, *anywhere in the world,* and give a talk or teach you and some of your friends *about the gospel message and these redemption realities,* simply contact us at www.livingwordintl.com …or you can always find me on www.facebook.com

If your life has changed as a result of reading this book, *please write to me and let me know.*

I would love to share in your joy,

…so that my joy in writing this series of books may be full!

"That which was from the beginning,

which we have heard
(with our spiritual ears),
which we have seen
(with our spiritual eyes),
which we have looked upon
(beheld, focused our attention upon),
and which our hands have also handled
(which we have also experienced),

concerning the Word of life,

we declare to you,

that you also may have this
fellowship with us;

and truly our fellowship is with
the Father
and with His Son Jesus Christ.

And these things we write to you
that your joy may be full.
 ~ 1John 1:1-4

About the Author

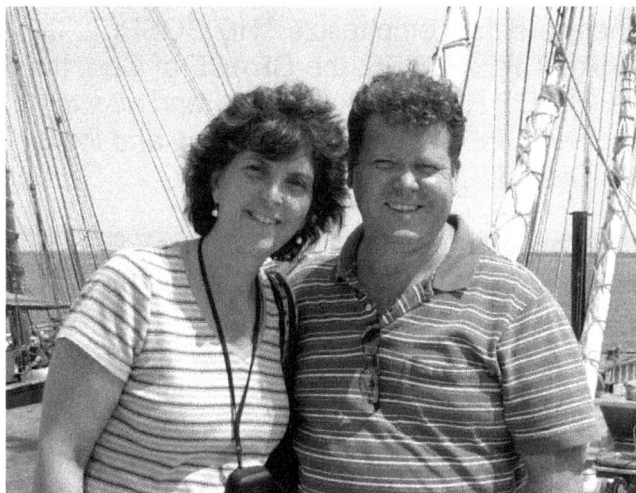

Rudi & Carmen Louw together oversee: Living Word International.

They also travel and minister both locally and internationally.

Rudi was born and raised in the country of South Africa, while Carmen grew up in Cortland, New York.

They function in the ministry of reconciliation (2 Corinthians 5:18-21) and flow strongly with the Holy Spirit and His anointing to teach, preach, prophesy, heal, *and whatever is needed to touch people's lives **with the reality of God's love and power.***

God has given them keen insight into what He has to say to mankind in the work of redemption *concerning the revelation and restoration of humanity's true identity.*

Therefore they emphasize THE GOSPEL, IN CHRIST REALITIES, the GRACE of God, the WORD OF RIGHTEOUSNESS, *and all such eternal truths essential to salvation and living the CHRIST-LIFE.*

They have been granted this wisdom and revelation into the knowledge of God by the resurrected Spirit of Jesus Christ, *to establish and strengthen believers in the faith of God, and to activate them in ministering to others.*

Not only are people set free from the poison and bondage of sin, condemnation and all kinds of intimidation, (upheld, strengthened and reinforced by age old religious ideas born out of ignorance) **but many are brought into a closer more intimate relationship with Father God, as Daddy**, through accurate teaching and unveiling of the gospel message, prophetic words, healings and miracles.

Rudi & Carmen are closely knitted together with many other effective Christians, church fellowships, and groups of believers who share the same revelation and passion **to impart the truth of the gospel to others, so as to impact and transform the world we live in with the LOVE and POWER of God.**

www.ingramcontent.com/pod-product-compliance
Lightning Source LLC
Chambersburg PA
CBHW060808050426
42449CB00008B/1594